What The Dark Could Not Keep

What The Dark Could Not Keep

a conversation about suicide

Pascal Comvalius
Jasmine Garg Sadiyah Reyal

Cover illustration by Jasmine Garg
Design by Studio Juno
Published by BoekenGilde

ISBN 978-9-46-526821-7

1for2socialinnovation.com
Boekengilde.nl

SOCIAL 1FOR2 INNOVATION

“ The light at the end of the tunnel is not an illusion; the tunnel is ”
Anna Quindlen

“ The light inside the darkness forever glows
The sun is like the diamond inside the coal
And like an embryo, it grows and grows and grows and grows ”
Prince

Table of Contents

Foreword

I first met Pascal in Las Vegas at a Hostage/Crisis Negotiators Conference, where, as the keynote speaker, I shared a story of an Afghan hostage negotiation case, which defined my life's purpose in helping others in crisis across the world. We are fortunate to share the same passion for teaching others in the craft of hostage/crisis negotiation, so I was honoured to contribute to this book.

We all have problems; our individual paths through life are all unique; no one has experienced what we have personally, so understanding a situation where another person wishes to end their life can often be overwhelming for many.

Suicide, often bluntly described as a permanent solution to a temporary problem, is complex and misunderstood by many. The chapters and personal stories in this book help us to gain a better understanding, to unravel the myths and to importantly give us confidence to intervene. I know from my own deep experience that, by talking with and empathically listening to a person in crisis, we can often affect behavioural change and guide them towards a better solution.

Often, as kind strangers, understanding how we can accompany others in their time of crisis is a vital life skill that allows us to embrace difference and, importantly, bring light where darkness reigns. Sometimes, we may not be successful in our intervention to help others, so equally, we must care for ourselves when this happens.

Thank you to the authors, Pascal, Jasmine and Sadiyah. I am encouraged by this book, which should help many of us, armed with a little courage, to sow the seeds of hope where despair seems dominant and help our fellow humans.

Andrew Brown
16 March 2026

Preface

After finishing my first book, Mediation in Criminal Cases, in 2022, I was hesitant for a long time to write another, even though I had told everyone one was in the works. That hesitation melted when Jasmine Garg, one of the co-authors of this book, was considering writing about her experience of suicide ideation. The feeling was further fuelled after following the course at the Dutch suicide helpline 113. Although there are many books about suicide and people who have attempted it, I thought it would be a good opportunity to have a conversation in book form about suicide from both a caregiver's perspective and that of a person who has attempted suicide. And here it is.

The book does not claim to be the ultimate book. It serves more as a practical guide for those acting as gatekeepers and for understanding the person considering ending their life. All thoughts and comments are primarily based on research, studies and interviews. The cover image is based on a painting by Benitsevich Leonid. It symbolises themes of an emotional rollercoaster, losing control, being sucked into a dark place, and being submerged in a hopeless situation. A vortex that picks you up and drops you somewhere else. It is known that at some point, a tornado or whirlpool will lose power, providing an opportunity to escape the danger zone. That is what this book also wants to give: another path. Suicide is not a choice. It is an illness that lives inside the soul and sets out to destroy the body.

Pascal Comvalius, The Hague, Netherlands, March 2026

Ethical considerations

Since real stories have been used, all examples have been stripped of any data that could identify clients personally to ensure full GDPR compliance. Please keep in mind that every situation involving suicide or an attempt is unique. It is not necessarily a one-size-fits-all format we are presenting. Assisted AI has been used for edits, grammar, and research. The authors have written the actual content.

Disclaimer

- Trigger warning: This book contains discussions about suicide, which may be distressing or triggering for some individuals.
- If you feel uncomfortable or need support at any given moment, please prioritise your well-being. Consider stepping away, reaching out to someone you trust, or contacting a mental health professional or helpline in your area.
- Your mental health matters, and it is okay to take care of yourself.

1 What is a crisis?

A crisis is a psychological state in which a person's usual coping skills stop working. For people who want to commit suicide, their methods for managing stress, regulating emotions, or resolving problems no longer provide needed relief. As a result, the person may feel overwhelmed, trapped, or unable to cope. The situation no longer seems manageable. Instead, it feels like a grave threat to their emotional well-being and can result in a dramatic decision.

During a suicidal crisis, behaviour is often driven by intense emotions that take over the logical thought process. Feelings such as fear, despair, shame, anger, or hopelessness can hamper the ability to reason or evaluate options. The ability to solve the issues they are dealing with and the lack of concentration are declining, making suicide seem like the only way to escape distress.

Crises often derive from a recent triggering event, usually within the past 24 hours. The trigger may be caused by external factors, such as a loss, conflict, or perceived failure, or by internal factors, such as a surge of painful emotions or thoughts. The impact will increase if the resources which we use to cope with these stressful events are already exhausted.

In such moments, the individual seeks relief from emotional tension. If safe, supportive outlets are unavailable, suicidal thoughts or actions may occur as an attempt to escape the crisis, but this does not imply that there is a true wish to die.

This perspective on a suicidal crisis emphasises that we need to be compassionate instead of being judgmental. It recognises that a crisis is a transient yet serious condition that requires immediate containment, support and help rebuilding the skills to cope with these situations. Recognising signs such as emotional overwhelm, impaired thinking, recent triggers, and diminished problem-solving enables caregivers and professionals to intervene more effectively, promoting safety and helping the individual find stability and hope in their life.

Cognitive conflict refers to the mental struggle that occurs when a person faces important choices with uncertain outcomes, especially if the consequences are serious. Here, 'cognitive conflict' means being torn between competing options. This leads to uncertainty and stress. When people must make decisions that truly matter but are unsure of the outcome or feel unable to control the results, they experience significant stress and emotional discomfort. Janis and Mann (1977) found that the Cognitive Conflict theory of decision making defines ongoing or unresolved conflict as persistent uncertainty between alternatives. This can interfere with clear thinking and lead to unhelpful coping strategies, especially when someone feels stuck between options they consider unacceptable. Regarding suicide, this theory is relevant. Those experiencing suicidal thoughts often face critical life decisions during times of great uncertainty. For example, they may wonder if their pain and emotional suffering will ever improve, which can increase cognitive conflict. When stress becomes overwhelming, it can create feelings of hopelessness, indecision, or a desire to escape. This can potentially raise the risk of suicidal behaviour.

2 What is suicide?

Shneidman's (1985) definition of suicide is best understood as a self-induced annihilation as a move toward the complete stopping of one's consciousness and unendurable pain, making it for the person who is suffering the best possible solution for all the pressing issues that they have. "Pain is the core of suicide. Suicide is an exclusively human response to extreme psychological pain."

Suicide is different from assisted dying, also known as "medical aid in dying (MAID)". They both involve intentionally ending a life due to extreme suffering or emotional distress. There are three core differences, however, that set them apart. Firstly, in legality. Where, for example, in the Netherlands, medical aid in dying is allowed and regulated under Dutch law. Secondly, in medical oversight, the drugs are prescribed by doctors after multiple conversations and with the written consent of the person. This process is formalised for the terminally ill themselves and the person who wants to die, to take the prescriptions themselves. Thirdly, suicide is often impulsive and driven by despair or untreated mental illness.

Having outlined the distinction between suicide and MAID, it is also valuable to consider what people who are suicidal tend to have in common. Suicidal people often experience frustrated psychological needs, unbearable psychological pain, helplessness, and hopelessness. For them, death is seen as a solution to end the suffering and the confusing emotions and feelings. In their opinion, there are only two solutions: living with the pain or ending it by taking their own life. Last but not least, suicidal people tend to have a history of prior suicide attempts combined with a hard time coping with the mental pressure they feel.

Summary Table of Key Differences

Feature	Assisted Dying / MAID	Suicide
Primary Condition	Terminal, incurable illness	Often, a mental health crisis/distress
Legal Status	Legal in specific jurisdictions	Generally illegal (or unauthorised)
Process	Regulated, two-doctor assessment	Often impulsive/ unregulated
Mental Capacity	Confirmed as competent	Often impaired by depression/distress
Involvement	Physician prescribes/ administers	Typically done alone

2.1 Myths and facts about suicide

Misunderstandings about suicide are widespread and can unintentionally heighten risk by discouraging the so much-needed open conversation, delaying the crucial help-seeking, and reinforcing stigma. Both Shneidman (1996) and Joiner (2005) emphasise that the myths around suicide are not harmless. The myths shape perception and attitudes, influence responses, and can determine whether someone in distress is met with support or silence. It is important for the public to distinguish between myths and facts; this is therefore a critical task for caregivers, gatekeepers and other professionals to educate the public regarding suicide.

One persistent myth is that talking about suicide will put the idea into someone's head. Clinical experience, as Sharma (2024) clearly explains, clearly contradicts this belief. Asking about suicide does not increase suicidal thoughts or behaviours; instead, it often reduces distress by giving individuals permission to speak openly about feelings they may have been carrying alone and helps people to find an alternative view of their existing issues (Gould et al., 2003). Talking about suicide in a calm, respectful, and direct way can help people feel heard, validated, and less isolated. Silence, avoidance, or dismissiveness, by contrast, can intensify feelings of alienation and despair. If we open the conversation, it will increase the likelihood that a person will seek treatment.

Another misconception is that suicide occurs suddenly and without warning. Shneidman (1993) argues that while some crises can escalate quickly, suicide usually results from a gradual process involving increasing stress, emotional pain, and a reduced sense of options.

Similar to this is the myth that people who talk about suicide are just seeking attention. In fact, many individuals who take their own lives have expressed their distress beforehand, either directly or indirectly. It is always important to take it seriously when somebody talks about feeling suicidal. Joiner (2005) found signs like saying goodbye to people as if they will not be seen again, expressing a desire not to live, feeling hopeless about the future, or believing they are a burden, and even the increase in the use of alcohol or drugs are well-known warning signals.

There is also a widespread myth that only people with mental illness are suicidal. Although conditions such as depression, anxiety, or trauma-related disorders definitely increase risk, the World Health Organisation (2014) states that suicide affects people of all ages and backgrounds, including those without a formal psychiatric diagnosis. Suicide is one of the leading causes of death worldwide and represents a serious public health problem with devastating consequences for families, workplaces, schools, and communities. Risk is often shaped by a combination of factors like mental health challenges, social isolation, loss, identity crises, and situational stressors instead of one single cause.

Another damaging myth is that people who die by suicide are selfish, cowardly, or weak. An overwhelming psychological pain drives suicidal behaviour and feels like the only solution, which Shneidman (1996) calls psychache, a desperate desire for relief rather than a lack of character or moral strength. Similarly, the belief that talk therapy or medication does not work is a myth. While no intervention is universally effective, Beck et al. (1979) and Stanley and Brown (2012) discovered that evidence-based psychological therapies, medication, and psychosocial support significantly contribute to the reduction of suicidal ideation and improve quality of life for many individuals.

The facts are that suicide can be prevented, the resources are available, and recovery from suicide ideation or a suicide attempt is possible. Many people facing suicidal crises can find a purpose in their lives again when they receive the right understanding, support, and the right kind of care. Eliminating the myths around suicide helps caregivers and communities to respond with compassion rather than judgment, and with proactivity rather than avoidance.

3 The law and suicide

By Sadiyah Reyal

"The surface of the Earth is the shore of the cosmic ocean. From it we have learned most of what we know. Recently, we have waded a little out to sea, enough to dampen our toes or, at most, wet our ankles. The water seems inviting. The ocean calls. Some part of our being knows this is from where we came. We long to return."
Carl Sagan, Cosmos (1980)

Consider what the universe has made of us.

We are, each of us, made of the same matter as ancient stars. The calcium in our bones, the iron in our blood, the carbon in every cell. All of it forged in stellar furnaces billions of years ago. Carl Sagan viewed this not as an abstraction, but as a claim about worth. About what we owe one another on this small, improbable planet.

If every person alive is a temporary gathering of star-stuff, briefly conscious, capable of suffering and love in equal measure, then what we owe one another is not a small thing. It is, perhaps, everything.

Against that backdrop, consider what the law has done.

There is a man in Gambia. He stabbed himself three times in the stomach after a painful break-up. After being treated in hospital, he was arrested, taken to court, convicted, and fined the equivalent of eighty US dollars. When he could not pay, he faced six months in prison. He was not treated as someone in crisis; instead, he was treated as a criminal (Adinkrah, 2016).

Now consider a woman in India. She survived a suicide attempt in 2019. Under the country's colonial-era penal code, she too could have been prosecuted. But India's Mental Healthcare Act, passed in 2017 and fully reinforced by the Bharatiya Nyaya Sanhita in 2024, says something different. It says she is presumed to be under severe stress. It says she shall not be tried or punished. It says the government has a duty to provide her with care, treatment, and rehabilitation (Vadlamani & Gowda, 2019).

Two people. The same unbearable pain. The same desperate reaching for something that might make it stop. What happens next depends almost entirely on the country they happen to live in.

This chapter examines what the law says about suicide around the world, not as a dry survey of statutes, but as a reflection of what societies believe about suffering, dignity, and who deserves to be helped. In the context of suicide, the law either protects the person in crisis or punishes them. Understanding what it does and why matters deeply for anyone working as a caregiver, a gatekeeper, or simply as a human being trying to reach someone in the dark.

3.1 A legacy built on punishment

To understand why so many countries still criminalise suicide attempts, we have to go back further than most people expect. The legal prohibition of suicide was not invented by governments, but rather was born in theology.

Saint Augustine, writing in the fifth century, argued that the commandment 'thou shalt not kill' applied to oneself (Augustine, 2003). That single argument became the foundation for centuries of ecclesiastical condemnation and, eventually, criminal sanction. English common law formalised the concept of felo de se (the self-murderer) under which suicide was treated as an offence against the Crown. Property could be forfeited, and burial in consecrated ground could be denied. The logic was blunt: your life belongs not to you, but to God and to the state.

What is less widely understood is how thoroughly this legal architecture was then exported. When Britain colonised large parts of Africa, Asia, and the Caribbean, it embedded its anti-suicide provisions into local penal codes. When independence came, those codes remained. Adinkrah (2016) documents this clearly in his study of nine African countries, noting that "a large number of the jurisdictions where attempted suicide is illegal comprise former British colonial territories". Countries where laws imposed during colonial governance are still enforced today. The bitter irony is that Britain repealed its own Suicide Act in 1961, with Parliament explicitly noting that the continuation of the offence was an obstacle to humane and remedial treatment. Many of its former colonies were not extended the same courtesy.

Think about what that means for a moment. A man in Gambia can be imprisoned under a law that the country that wrote it no longer believes in. The colonisers moved on, but their laws stayed.

As of 2024, twenty-three countries still criminalise suicide attempts under their criminal justice systems, including Kenya, Nigeria, Bangladesh, Uganda, and several Caribbean nations, with an additional twenty applying punishment through Sharia law frameworks (Mishara & Weisstub, 2016; Wu et al., 2024).

3.2 The effects of criminalisation

The most common defence of laws that criminalise suicide attempts is deterrence: the idea that the threat of legal consequences prevents people from attempting suicide. Although the claim is often made and with great confidence, the evidence does not support it.

Wu et al. (2022) conducted an ecological study across 171 countries and found that criminalisation of suicide was associated with slightly increased national suicide rates, instead of decreased. The harmful association was strongest among women in lower-income countries, suggesting that punitive laws interact with patriarchal social structures in ways that leave the most vulnerable people more exposed, not less. The authors concluded that alternative approaches should be considered: providing quality mental healthcare and addressing the socioeconomic and cultural factors that contribute to suicide.

A second effect is more intuitive once you hear it. Criminalisation may push people toward choosing more lethal methods, specifically to avoid the possibility of surviving an attempt only to face imprisonment and societal stigma (Agyapong et al., 2022; Lew et al., 2022). A law designed to prevent death may be making death more likely, because surviving becomes the thing that is punished.

There is also the silence. Agyapong et al. (2022) argue that criminalisation significantly hinders help-seeking, because people conceal their suicidal thoughts specifically because they fear legal consequences. And when suicides go unreported or misclassified, governments cannot build accurate prevention programmes. The deterrence argument, already weak, rests on a foundation of data that the law itself corrupts.

Perhaps the most striking illustration of this comes from Malaysia. Despite having laws that were rarely enforced in practice, a forensic study found that between 2008 and 2019, twenty-two people with mental illness were prosecuted for attempted suicide, and for most of them, it was their first-ever contact with any mental health service (Ng & Panirselvam, 2021). A law does not need to be consistently enforced to cause harm; its existence alone shapes whether a person in crisis believes it is safe to reach out.

The Lancet summarised the situation plainly in 2023: in over twenty countries, a person recovering in hospital after a suicide attempt may face prosecution once they leave medical care; in effect, punished for not killing themselves (The Lancet, 2023).

3.3 When does the law protect?

India represents the most significant recent positive shift in this landscape. The Mental Healthcare Act of 2017 did something remarkable: it created a legal presumption that any person who attempts suicide is under severe stress, cannot be prosecuted, and must be provided with care and rehabilitation by the government. And in July 2024, the Bharatiya Nyaya Sanhita fully replaced the colonial Indian Penal Code, removing the old criminalisation provision entirely, completing what Vadlamani and Gowda (2019) describe as one of the most significant shifts in how the law relates to mental health in any country in the world.

Ghana decriminalised in 2023, following a sustained parliamentary debate in which lawyers and judges argued that people who had attempted suicide should be treated as patients rather than criminals. That decision is already influencing reform conversations in Grenada, Sierra Leone, and Nigeria. Osafo et al. (2024) carefully document this momentum, noting that successful reform requires sustained engagement with religious leaders, healthcare workers, and communities, not just legislators.

The United for Global Mental Health advocacy guide (2025) captures what this shift looks like in practice: countries that decriminalise tend to see improved reporting, better surveillance of suicidal behaviour, and more people willing to access services. The goal of decriminalisation, as the guide emphasises, is not merely the passing of legislation. It is the creation of conditions in which someone in the darkest moment of their life believes that reaching out will lead to care, not consequence.

3.4 The hardest legal question: when is intervention forced?

Criminalisation is the most visible legal injustice in the global landscape, and involuntary detention is the most morally complex.

In most countries, a person assessed as at imminent risk of suicide can be detained in a psychiatric facility without their consent. In the United States, a seventy-two-hour hold can be initiated based on evidence of danger to self or others. In Japan, there is no specified time limit. In Brazil, a family member can authorise hospitalisation. In Korea, family consent has historically been central to compulsory admission. The threshold and the process vary enormously, but the underlying structure is consistent: a person with a mental health diagnosis can be detained preventively, before any act is committed, in a way that a person without such a diagnosis cannot.

Szmukler (2020) identifies the discrimination at the heart of this: "the autonomy or right to self-determination is not respected as it is for others, those who do not have a mental disorder diagnosis." The UN Convention on the Rights of Persons with Disabilities (2006) has further sharpened this tension. Its Committee has interpreted Article 12 and Article 14 as prohibiting involuntary detention on the grounds of disability, which would place most of the world's existing mental health legislation, including England's Mental Health Act, in direct conflict with international human rights standards (Szmukler et al., 2014).

Northern Ireland has attempted to resolve this tension through what legal scholars call a 'Fusion Law': a single capacity-based framework that applies the same standards to everyone, regardless of whether the cause of impaired decision-making is a mental illness, a physical injury, or something else entirely. It is the most advanced legislative response to this paradox currently in existence. Whether the rest of the world will follow is another question.

For caregivers and gatekeepers, this tension arrives in the sharpest possible way in the clinical moment: do I detain this person, disrupting the trust we have built, or do I keep them in the community and risk a different outcome? The evidence from Stanley et al. (2012) and Bryan et al. (2017) suggests that safety planning, built collaboratively with the person in crisis, is more effective in the long term than coercive containment. But legal liability shapes what clinicians feel they can safely do. Saya et al. (2025) document how the rising incidence of malpractice suits for patient suicide is driving defensive over-hospitalisation across Europe and North America, even when clinical judgement points toward a less restrictive approach. The law shapes what happens in the room, not just in the courtroom.

3.5 The law and medical aid in dying

Medical Aid in Dying (MAID) occupies a different part of this legal landscape, and it is worth being precise about that difference, because the terminology matters as much as the substance.

As discussed earlier in this book, MAID and suicide are legally and clinically distinct. All American MAID statutes explicitly define these deaths as not constituting suicide for the purposes of death certificates and insurance policies. The terminological debate, physician-assisted suicide versus death with dignity versus medical aid in dying, is not merely semantic. The language used, as the American Psychiatric Association's Resource Guide acknowledges, colours the underlying moral and legal perspectives (Gunther et al., 2024).

As of 2025, MAID is legal in the Netherlands, Belgium, Canada, Switzerland, Germany, Spain, New Zealand, Australia, Colombia, and several US states (covering more than one-fifth of the American population). The conditions under which it is permitted, however, vary significantly across jurisdictions. In most systems, eligibility is limited to individuals with a serious and incurable medical condition, often accompanied by advanced and irreversible decline and intolerable suffering. Some jurisdictions, including the Netherlands and Belgium, permit MAID in cases of non-terminal illness, and, in rare and highly regulated circumstances, for psychiatric conditions. Others, such as many US states and Australia, restrict access to those with a terminal illness and a defined prognosis, typically requiring that death be expected within six or twelve months. Across all jurisdictions, common safeguards include capacity assessments, voluntariness requirements, and multiple independent medical evaluations, reflecting an attempt to distinguish enduring, autonomous choice from decisions made in acute crisis. But what qualifies as "intolerable suffering", and who is authorised to define it?

Canada's trajectory has attracted particular attention. From terminal illness in 2016, to non-terminal suffering in 2021, to mental illness as a sole qualifying condition planned for 2024, Canada moved faster than any comparable jurisdiction. A Special Joint Committee concluded in early 2024 that accurately distinguishing whether a mental illness is irremediable and whether a request reflects genuine autonomous will or suicidality remained problems unlikely to be resolved in the foreseeable future (Journal of the American Academy of Psychiatry and the Law, 2024). Canada subsequently delayed implementation until March 2027.

The contrast that MAID illuminates is uncomfortable but important. A terminally ill person in Belgium may legally request a medically assisted death. A person in Kenya who survives a suicide attempt may be arrested. Both are expressing a wish to die. What determines their legal fate is the diagnosis attached to their suffering and the country in which they live. This is not a simple equivalence; MAID involves careful clinical assessment, capacity evaluation, and multi-step oversight that an acute crisis does not. But the contrast exposes something worth sitting with: the same underlying act is treated as a right in one legal category and a crime in another. That incoherence asks something of us.

3.6 What does the law do to families?

As you would expect, legal consequences do not end with the person who has died.

In England, Wales, and many common law jurisdictions, a death by suicide triggers a mandatory coronial investigation and often a public inquest. The inquest takes place in a courtroom, is open to the media, and typically occurs four to twelve months after the death. For this entire period, the family exists in a protracted, institutionalised form

of grief. The death cannot be formally registered until the inquest concludes, which means estates cannot be administered, insurance claims cannot be initiated, and in some systems, the body cannot be released for burial without a coroner's order (UKSOBS, 2024).
Most life insurance policies globally include a suicide exclusion clause, typically covering the first one to two years of the policy. Families bereaved by suicide may therefore face both grief and sudden financial exposure simultaneously, at the moment in their lives when they are least equipped to manage either. Where MAID deaths are explicitly defined as non-suicide in law, those families are protected from these exclusions. The same underlying act, a deliberate choice to die, is insurable in one legal category and not in another.

The psychological literature on suicide bereavement is clear about the stakes. Jordan and McIntosh (2011) found that people bereaved by suicide are at greater risk for depressive disorders, post-traumatic stress, and suicidal ideation themselves. A legal system that adds bureaucratic trauma to grief - the unanswered phone calls, the coroner's court, the insurance forms, the waiting - is not a neutral system. It is one that adds harm to harm.

3.7 What does good law look like?

Optimistically, the direction of travel globally is toward decriminalisation, rights-based mental health frameworks, and a recognition of suicide as a public health emergency that requires care rather than punishment. The WHO's Comprehensive Mental Health Action Plan (2013–2030) makes this explicit, calling on governments to develop national suicide prevention strategies, reform legislation, and remove barriers to help-seeking. As of 2023, only thirty-eight countries have such strategies in place (WHO, 2023).

Four things define what good law in this field looks like. First, full decriminalisation of suicide attempts, with a legal presumption of distress rather than culpability. Second, a statutory government obligation to provide care after an attempt - not an aspiration, but an enforceable right, as India has demonstrated. Third, mental health legislation that treats involuntary detention as a genuine last resort, time-limited, independently reviewed, and grounded in capacity assessment rather than diagnosis alone. Fourth, legal protections for bereaved families, trauma-informed processes, insurance rights, and access to clear information when it is needed most.

None of this, on its own, saves a life. Law creates conditions, and it removes barriers. It signals what a society believes about the value of a person in pain. But what actually reaches someone in the darkest moment is what every other chapter of this book addresses: trust, empathy, presence, and the willingness to stay. The man in Gambia and the woman in India were not asking for a statute. They were asking for someone to stay.

The law can stop punishing despair. What it cannot do is replace the person willing to sit beside someone in it; willing, in Sagan's words, to make the vastness bearable.

"For small creatures such as we
the vastness is bearable only through love."
Carl Sagan, Contact (1985)

4 The road to an increasing risk of suicide

As discussed in the previous chapters, suicide does not happen unexpectedly. It is more common that the path to a higher suicide risk develops slowly, characterised by evolving thought patterns, emotional states, and life experiences that accumulate over time. So it is important to detect and understand this progress and to intervene as the psychological distress can intensify rapidly.

Worrying is often one of the first feelings people experience on this road. It involves a chain of thoughts mixed with negative feelings, usually centred around potential future threats. Worry tends to steer our minds toward imagined dangers, losses, or failures. While it is entirely normal to worry from time to time, Borkovec et al. (1983) found that persistent worry can become a cycle of anxiety, making the future feel more overwhelming and beyond our control. Worry starts first in all its innocence. As worry deepens, it can lead to rumination. Rumination can be characterised by repetitive negative thoughts and emotions focused on depressive symptoms and their perceived consequences, according to Nolen-Hoeksema (1991). Individuals who ruminate tend to fixate on difficulties and distressing memories, repeatedly replay past events, and become absorbed with unresolved problems. Although rumination is often learned as a coping mechanism or problem-solving strategy, it often comes back like a boomerang, and the emotional pain starts to increase instead of being eased. It will also strengthen feelings of self-blame and helplessness.

A deep sense of anguish can even establish if ongoing worry and rumination develop over time. This kind of suffering goes beyond just physical pain; it deeply impacts a person's emotional and mental state. It can show up in various forms, such as intense grief, lingering remorse, or a constant feeling of despair that seems impossible to escape. Anguish does not stay limited to just sadness. What anguish can do is take over your thoughts and emotions. Not even your body is safe. It acts like a tsunami, with brutal force, destroying everything in its path. Physically, you might notice lingering pain, tenderness, heaviness, constant crying, slowed movement, reduced energy, or a strong urge to sleep. At an emotional and psychological level, it may prompt you to question who you are, your core beliefs, your purpose, or your place in the world. Sometimes, deeper existential worries surface, leaving you feeling more disconnected and lacking a sense of meaning.

To understand what anguish visually would look like, Munch's (1893) painting called *"The Scream"* gives you a good idea. It has often been described as a soul laid bare and a painting of the inner psychological landscape and suffering, where his own suicidal thoughts and despair are portrayed.

When emotional distress lasts a long time, especially if you are dealing with a chronic illness or ongoing mental health struggles, it can affect more than just how you feel inside. Your quality of life might take a hit as physical abilities decline and social ties weaken. Often, social connections do not notice at first that their social contact is declining.

When a person in crisis thinks that pulling away from loved ones and activities is the best thing they can do, it hurts their self-esteem and sense of worth even more, making them feel like a burden or like they are nobody's value.

If this situation continues, it might become even more overwhelming, especially given the person in crisis's isolation. Feelings of deep sorrow or grief can linger, along with a sense of hopelessness or despair that does not go away. Physical pain might float to the surface and is more prominent along with emotional pain, leading to feelings of exhaustion and being drained. As these feelings grow, people may notice themselves withdrawing more from others and struggling with daily tasks that once felt manageable.

At this point, the risk of suicide may become more apparent or grow stronger. This is the immediate danger zone. Feelings of wanting to escape from their world, find relief, or end the pain might start to feel and sound more like a solution, especially when the future seems empty, all hope is gone, and only despair remains, and the current situation feels and stays overwhelming. In the end, suicide is not caused by just one thing, as mentioned earlier, but usually results from ongoing suffering, limited ability to think, and feeling like there are no options left.

Recognising the signs that someone is heading toward increased risk gives us a chance to step in early before despair takes hold. By easing worries, breaking rumination patterns, acknowledging feelings of anguish, and helping rebuild connection and purpose, not only with the help of caregivers or gatekeepers but also loved ones, family, friends, and even colleagues at work can change this course. Understanding these signs is not about predicting what will happen, but about catching suffering early and responding with compassion, support, and hope to show the people in despair that there is a way out.

For what a person can handle in a crisis, each person has a different tolerance window. Understanding the window can foster empathy, according to Siegel (1999). When people operate within this window, they can handle the difficulties and challenges of life with greater resilience. But if they step outside of those boundaries, they might feel overwhelmed or numb. This is especially applicable to people who are struggling with past trauma or ongoing stress. For individuals who consider committing suicide, this window can be so narrowed that everyday tasks or experiences, like getting out of bed or rejection, become unbearable. It is important to view these reactions not as deliberate choices but as responses to a nervous system overwhelmed beyond its capacity.

4.1 Attachment and its relationship to suicidal behaviour

Attachment is defined by Bowlby (1969) as: "the emotional bonds formed with primary caregivers early in life, which shape internal working models of self-worth, emotional regulation, and expectations of support from others." Insecure attachment styles, particularly anxious and avoidant attachment, are associated with an increased risk of suicidal ideation and behaviour. It was found by Mikulincer and Shaver (2012) that, on one hand, individuals with anxious attachment may experience intense fear of abandonment, heightened emotional distress, and dependency, which can amplify feelings of hopelessness during interpersonal crises, on the other hand, those with avoidant attachment often suppress emotional needs, avoid seeking help, and experience profound isolation, all of which are significant risk factors for suicidal behaviour. In the research of Adam et al. (1996), it became clear that insecure attachment is also linked to impaired emotion regulation, negative self-concept, and difficulty forming supportive relationships, reducing protective factors against suicide. The research of Sheftall et al. (2014) suggests that secure attachment is associated with better coping strategies, stronger social support, and lower suicide risk, highlighting the importance of relational safety and emotional connectedness in suicide prevention efforts.

4.2 Suicide ideation among Generation Z and Generation Alpha

Suicide ideation has existed for generations. Unfortunately, Witt et al. (2025) found that there is a noticeable increase in suicide ideation among both Generation Z and Alpha. But what is causing this?

First, it is important to understand the characteristics of both generations. Katz et al. (2021) explain that Generation Z, people born between 1997 and 2012, is the first generation to have never known a world without Wi-Fi, the internet, cell phones, and social media. They often self-educate and are influenced by prevailing trends in the digital world. Generation Alpha, people born between 2012 and mid-2020, are growing up in an even more interconnected world in which artificial intelligence is increasingly prevalent. In many Western countries, Generation Alpha is projected to be the most racially and ethnically diverse generation to date, including diversity in family structure (single parents, blended families, same-sex parents). This normalises pluralism and inclusion as default social conditions rather than emerging social shifts.

Even though these generations prioritise a work-life balance, value inclusivity, diversity, social justice and are open about mental health challenges, they are more vulnerable to a mental health crisis. Academic pressure and competitive labour markets, economic uncertainty, political polarisation, climate change, wars, and the COVID-19 pandemic have caused and continue to take a toll on these generations. The COVID-19 pandemic, in particular, disrupted social interactions during adolescence. This caused an increase in persistent sadness and hopelessness among high school students. They also felt lonelier, which is one of the strongest predictors of depression and suicide ideation. Twenge et al. (2018) found correlations between heavy social media use and depressive symptoms, particularly among girls. Cyberbullying, social comparison, body image pressure and exposure to self-harm content increase the risk as well. The role of influencers can not be underestimated either.

Witt et al. (2025) note that the heightened exposure to suicide in peers or family, online content showing self-harm, and witnessing violence appear to be stronger predictors in younger cohorts than some traditional risk factors seen in older generations. Preliminary data indicate that more than one-quarter of Gen Alpha teens report having had a mental health problem, and that many value open discussion of mental health, which could influence help-seeking behaviours (Springtide, 2025).

5 Recognising potential signs of suicidal risk

The earlier we recognise and understand the potential signs that someone may be considering suicide as a solution to their problems, the better we are able to prevent this person from following up on this. Both Shneidman (1996) and Joiner (2005) found that suicide is never unexpected. It is a development that has recognisable patterns in behavioural changes, life circumstances, and communication. One single behaviour is never the defined pattern on the road to suicide. Therefore, clusters of behaviour are needed in our findings. Recognising them does not mean assuming intent, but it does mean taking concern seriously and responding with care, curiosity, and support.

O'Connor (2011) refers to suicide ideation as: "a spectrum of thoughts, wishes, and mental images related to death and self-harm, ranging from passive thoughts about not wanting to exist to active planning and attempts." This definition illustrates that suicidal behaviour can be best seen as a process rather than an act that happens suddenly. All models of suicide ideation emphasise progression over time, influenced by psychological pain, cognitive narrowing, a reduction in the width of the window of tolerance, personal factors, and access to means. As illustrated by the pyramid model of suicide ideation, experiences often move from less visible internal states at the base of the pyramid, such as thoughts and wishes, toward more visible and dangerous behaviours at the top, including preparation, attempts, and the suicide itself.

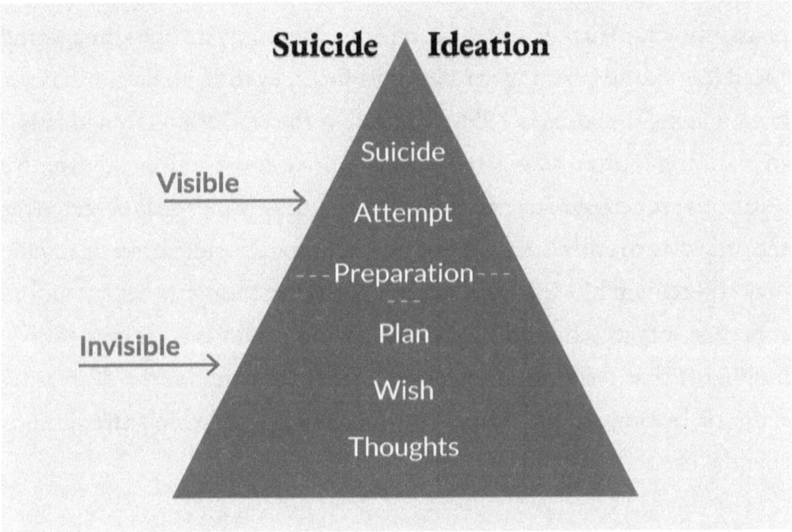

If we look at the pyramid, we also see that part of it cannot be noticed directly. It is like the pyramid is buried in the sand. At the lower, largely invisible levels of the pyramid, individuals may experience suicidal thoughts and wishes. These can include passive desires such as wishing to fall asleep and not wake up, or recurrent thoughts that life is no longer worth living. According to the cognitive theory of Beck et al. (1979), these thoughts are formed by negative core beliefs about the self, the world, and the future, often accompanied by feelings of hopelessness. Rumination and psychological pain, or psychache, play a vital role at this stage; Shneidman (1993) sees the unbearable psychological pain as a key driver of thinking about suicide. Although these thoughts may not be visible from the outside, they are markers of a significant internal struggle and represent increased vulnerability.

As the suicide ideation intensifies, individuals may begin to form plans, moving further up the pyramid. Planning involves imagining specific methods, timing, or circumstances, even if no action has yet been taken. Shneidman (1996) found that the transition from ideation to planning is often associated with cognitive constriction. Alternative solutions are out of reach, according to them, and suicide is perceived as the only way to end suffering. At this stage, the consideration of suicide may still remain hidden from others, but as the thoughts become more coherent, organised, and rehearsed, the risk increases. Joiner (2005) highlights that feelings of perceived burdensomeness and a decreasing sense of belonging can deepen during this phase, which strengthens suicidal desire.

The preparation stage marks a critical shift from thinking to doing and occupies the boundary between invisible and visible behaviour in the pyramid. Thoughts are now put into action. As part of their preparation, the person may start to give away their possessions, write (suicidal) notes, secure means, or choose a location. These behaviours are strong indicators that the person is moving closer to an attempt, even if the doubt on actually executing it remains. Shneidman (2001) shows that it is normal to feel ambivalent throughout the entire suicidal process. Preparation reflects an even narrower window of tolerance and increasing psychological commitment to suicide as a solution.

At the top of the pyramid are suicide attempts and suicide itself, which are the most visible outcomes of the ideation process. It is important to emphasise that people with suicidal thoughts do not automatically progress to an attempt. Stanley and Brown (2012) point out that protective factors, timely intervention, social connection, and restricted access to lethal means can interrupt this trajectory. Caregivers and gatekeepers have to understand that suicide ideation is a dynamic process, and if they recognise the signals of the crisis early, especially at the less visible stages, these moments are critical points for intervention. Addressing thoughts and wishes with empathy and seriousness can prevent progression upward, reinforcing the idea that suicide ideation is not a single event but a process that can be slowed, redirected, and, in many cases, stopped.

As explained earlier, one of the most common warning signs of suicide risk is a noticeable change in behaviour. A strong warning sign is social withdrawal. Beck et al. (1979) found that this is often accompanied by a loss of interest in activities that once provided meaning or pleasure, reflecting a broader disengagement from life and leading to avoidance of contact with friends, family, or colleagues.

Shneidman (1993) further indicates that people may also engage in risky, reckless behaviour without considering the consequences. It is also possible to see that people increase their use of alcohol or drugs and get themselves involved in dangerous activities. Such behaviours can indicate a diminished regard for personal safety and an escalation in psychological pain. Another important behaviour indicator to note is persistent sadness or a visibly low mood; this is particularly important when it is deep, enduring, and appears disproportionate to current circumstances. These behavioural shifts often signal intense internal distress that the individual may not yet be able or willing to articulate.

Both Beck et al (1979) and Shneidman (1996) found that another helpful indicator of suicidal ideation is the language that is being used. This can be from a verbal and a written perspective. The language can reveal profound despair, hopelessness, or a desire to escape unbearable pain. Sometimes these expressions are direct, such as stating "I wish I were dead" or saying "I can no longer endure this situation". In other cases, the language is indirect but equally concerning. It is important to ask clarifying questions to understand the expressions. Statements such as "I will not be bothering you anymore," "For me it is no longer necessary," or "Here, take this—I will not be needing it anymore" may suggest psychological withdrawal from life or preparatory behaviour. Expressions of entrapment and hopelessness, such as "What is the use of this?" or "I cannot see any way out of this," are strongly associated with suicidal ideation, particularly when accompanied by a belief that suffering will not end.

Anger and resentment may also appear in suicidal language. Phrases like "They will be sorry," "I will show them," or "Everybody hates me" can reflect a mixture of pain, shame, and a desire to be understood or to escape perceived rejection. Repeated expressions such as "No one understands," "This is too much for me," or "I would be better off dead" should always be taken seriously, even when expressed casually or framed as humour. These communications, as noted by Joiner (2005), may occur in conversations, text messages, social media posts, letters, or notes, and any recurring pattern of such language warrants attention and follow-up.

O'Connor (2011) suggests that certain life events and contextual factors can significantly increase vulnerability to suicidal thoughts. One of the strongest predictors of a risk in the future of a person wanting to commit suicide is a history of previous suicide attempts. This indicates that the person is familiar with suicidal behaviour and psychological distress, which has never been resolved. Recent losses, such as employment, a relationship, social status, financial struggles, or an identity crisis, can be the cause of overwhelmed coping mechanisms and will strengthen the feelings of helplessness. The death of a beloved family member or friend will also heighten the risk, as does exposure to suicide. The stronger the bond, the more intense the person's crisis. Last but not least are the underlying mental health conditions, such as depression, anxiety disorders, or trauma-related conditions.

As mentioned a couple of times before, there is no single sign that indicates that a person will attempt suicide. However, when behavioural changes, expressions of despair, and significant life stressors occur together, the level of concern should increase. As caregivers, we should see these signs as indicators of suffering rather than weakness or attention-seeking behaviour, according to Shneidman (1993).

Recognising warning signs creates an opportunity for connection and intervention. Asking direct questions, listening without judgment, and seeking help together can interrupt isolation and restore a sense of safety. Awareness does not require certainty; it requires compassion, attentiveness, and the willingness to act when someone's life may be at risk.

5.1 A story: My iron lung

Lisa wanted a change in her life. There was an aching, desperate need to escape the life she was living. Everything around her felt heavy, as if the world itself was pressing down on her. Depression, tangled with anxiety, made even the most minor changes feel overwhelming. Lisa wondered whether the world might be wrong, or whether she was seeing everything wrong in the world she lived in. Then she discovered that she was scared, not just of what was around her, but of her own mind.

Some days, her thoughts were sluggish, weighing her down and making it almost impossible to get out of bed. On other days, her mind raced uncontrollably. Her brain filled every quiet moment with noise. Noise that she could not stop and turn into silence. Even sunlight, once something she loved, began to feel harsh and unforgiving on her. One time when spring arrived, and the air grew softer, she told her parents she wanted to go out for some fresh air. Both of them were relieved. Believing that their daughter was finally emerging from the cold, dark space she had been trapped in and that happy days were ahead.

That afternoon, she sat behind the wheel of her father's car, driving toward the national highway. The engine murmured softly beneath her hands as the road stretched ahead, wide, open, and empty. For a while, the silence felt almost soothing. However, beneath it, a darker thought stirred.

When she reached the flyover, the idea crept in: a sharp turn to the right, just one move, and everything could end. No one else was on the road. It would be quick—nobody to save me. The pain would stop. After all, it was her life, so what would hold her back from taking her own life? She would not be hurting anyone else.

The sun poured through the windshield, warm against her skin. In normal circumstances, it should have comforted her. She had always loved the way spring replaced the cold winter. But not this year. Nothing seemed to reach her anymore. If even sunlight could not lift the weight inside her, what else could?

Her grip on the steering wheel in that moment tightened. The thought lingered, tempting and persistent. Nevertheless, then, another thought surfaced: the car was not hers. It belonged to her father. Lisa realised that she had already caused her parents so much pain. Did she have the right to hurt them more? Somehow, in that moment, the car seemed more valuable than her own life.

But she knew the truth. Her father would not grieve for the car. The grief would be for her being dead. Moreover, her mother would not cry over broken glass; she would cry over the daughter she could not save. Still, the thought echoed in her mind: *Is my life worth less than an old car?*

Her phone rang, breaking the silence. It was her mother. "Papa needs the car," she said softly. "When are you coming back?"

These words pulled Lisa back just enough. Her father needed the car. Moreover, maybe, in some small way, her parents still needed her. The weight on her heart did not disappear; it loosened just a little. She was glad she had not turned the wheel. At least for now, that was enough to keep going.

This was not just one isolated incident; there were many others. When Lisa was first diagnosed, her psychiatrist had urged her parents to lock away anything that could be used to harm herself, corrosive substances, ropes, and sharp objects. Even the medication she took had to be hidden from her and could only be taken under the supervision of one of the parents. She was actively suicidal then, and thoughts of ending it consumed every moment of her life. At times, she searched her home relentlessly, hoping to find something, anything, that could help her to escape the pain. But her parents were careful. They followed the doctor's advice to the letter.

Lisa was angry. How dare they force her to stay alive when they knew she was miserable? Keeping her physically safe only prolonged the torment in her mind. It felt cruel, like they were keeping her trapped in a life she no longer wanted to live.

One day, when the weight became too much to bear, Lisa grew desperate. Her mother was asleep. Her father had left for work. This was her chance. She decided she would take every pill she could find in the house, no matter what they were for. Mixed together, surely something would work. There had to be side effects. She tore through cupboards, drawers, kitchen shelves, the bathroom, anywhere her parents might have hidden them. But they had been thorough. Too thorough.

Still, she was not ready to give up. She woke her mother gently and told her she was going out to buy some snacks. Her mother, drowsy and unsuspecting, let her go. But Lisa had no intention of buying snacks. She drove to a nearby pharmacy, her plan sharp and clear in her mind.

She would ask for a refill of her mother's blood pressure and diabetes medication. She had invented new symptoms, anything to get her hands on more pills. They would not sell her sleeping tablets, but cough syrup was easier to get. She would buy two bottles and drink them all at once. The syrup would lull her into a deep sleep while the other pills quietly shut down her body. She even planned to fake a call home, pretending to check if her mother needed anything else. It would make her look less suspicious.

She sat in her car, rehearsing the perfect plan. But then she remembered the snacks. She had promised her mother to bring two of whatever she chose. Should she leave her waiting? What did it matter? Soon, none of it would matter.

Her thoughts spun wildly. In a moment of hesitation, she called her friend. Maybe, just maybe, talking would keep her from following through. But when her friend answered the cell phone, Lisa could not speak. It felt as if the pills were already lodged in her throat, choking her.

"Where are you?" her friend asked, sensing something was wrong.

“Out,” Lisa whispered.

“Out where?”

“I do not know. Just... out.”

“This does not sound good. What are you planning? Please, Lisa, go home.”

“I do not know what to do. I am tired... tired of pretending to be fine.”

“I know. But there will come a day when you will no longer have to pretend. You just have to hold on until then. Please, go home. I will call your mother if you do not.”

“No, do not tell her. Please, you have to let me...”

“I cannot. I know things can get better.”

Lisa’s voice trembled. “Okay... just give me a little time. I need to be sad for a while. I need to cry. Then I will go home.”

“Fine. But I am staying on the call until I hear your mom’s voice. If I do not, I am calling her myself.”

“Okay.”

And so she cried. Deep, wracking sobs shook her whole body. When the tears finally slowed, she drove back home. In her hands were two items of whatever she had grabbed from the store. After Lisa arrived home, she gave her parents a big hug. It made her realise that they were her iron lung, the life support that kept her moving.

6 Suicide risk assessment: another angle

Again, a chapter about the same topic? Yes and no. Yes, because it is about risk assessment regarding suicide again, no, because this assessment is a different model. It might be helpful to see which model serves you better as a gatekeeper or caregiver. This suicide risk assessment can be seen as an escalation ladder aimed at understanding the immediacy and seriousness of risk so that safety and the type of intervention can be prioritised. It is not about predicting outcomes with certainty, but about identifying factors that increase or reduce danger and responding appropriately. This effective assessment integrates three key elements: the *severity of suicidal thoughts and intent*, the person's *current mental state*, and the *lethality and accessibility of any plan*.

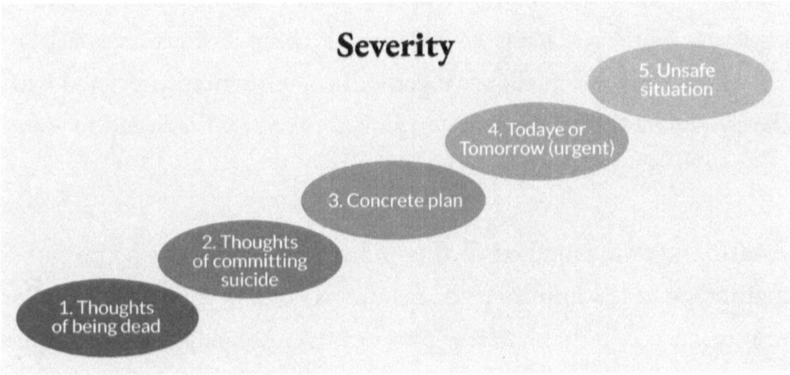

The image above illustrates a continuum of severity in suicidal risk. At the lower end are *thoughts of being dead*, often passive wishes such as wanting to disappear or not wake up. The risk increases when these thought processes shift to *thoughts of committing suicide*, where death becomes linked to self-harm. The next step in the escalation is the presence of a *concrete plan*. It is a significant step as it indicates a move from ideation towards action. When that plan is tied to a specific timeframe, such as *today or tomorrow*, the situation becomes urgent. At the highest level, an unsafe situation arises when multiple risk factors converge, requiring immediate intervention.

As severity increases, the plan's specificity becomes especially important. The more detailed a plan is, covering the how, when, and where, the higher the potential lethality. Vague ideas generally indicate a lower immediate risk than well-thought-out, rehearsed plans. Specificity signals preparation and intent, and therefore requires a more urgent response.

Linked to this is the method's lethality. Some methods carry a much higher risk of death than others. For example, the use of a firearm presents a significantly higher lethality than the ingestion of medication. Understanding the medical danger and consequences associated with the chosen method helps to determine how critical the situation is and what level of protection is needed.

Availability of the method further influences risk. Even a highly lethal method poses less immediate danger if it is not accessible, while easy or immediate access dramatically increases risk. A change in access, such as buying a gun or being alone with it, can rapidly escalate a situation from concerning to unsafe.

Another crucial factor is the proximity of a rescuer. Risk increases when a person is isolated or physically distant from others who could intervene. Being alone in a remote location where people cannot get to immediately, or in circumstances where discovery is unlikely, or having the caregiver, gatekeeper, family member, or friend on the phone increases lethality by reducing the chance of timely rescue or interruption.

Alongside these planning and lethality factors, assessing the person's current mental state provides essential context. Orientation is a key indicator: confusion about who or where they are can signal impaired judgment. The clarity and realism of thinking must also be considered, as distorted or rigid thinking can limit a person's ability to see alternatives to suicide.

The emotional state of mind plays a leading role. A combination of overwhelming, unstable, or incongruent emotions may provide you with the information that the person's capacity to regulate distress has been surpassed. Body movements and behaviour, such as agitation, extreme slowing, or bizarre gestures, can reflect severe internal distress. Sensory awareness may also be altered, with some individuals appearing numb, detached, or disconnected from their surroundings.

Awareness of other people is another protective factor to assess. When individuals lose sensitivity to how others might be affected, or feel completely disconnected from those around them, social buffers against suicide weaken. Finally, self-control is critical. Difficulty controlling thoughts, speech, or movements suggests a higher risk of impulsive action, particularly when combined with access to lethal means.

When high severity on the suicide continuum aligns with a specific and lethal plan, it is clear that everyone should be on high alert. Having immediate access to the means, isolation from family members, friends or caregivers, and impaired mental functioning is a recipe for the imminent attempt to commit suicide. In these situations, immediate safety measures, close supervision, and a warm handover to professional support are essential.

6.1 A story: I am not angry with you, life / Tuujhse naraaz nhi zindagi

Kabir has a profound theory about why individuals might harm themselves when grappling with mental illness. He believes that physical pain often serves to quiet the mind's anguish. The human body, it seems, can focus on only one kind of pain at a time, and when given a choice, one might prefer the tangible ache of the body over the invisible torment of the mind. This perspective underscores two important truths: first, we are inherently better equipped to handle physical pain, whether our own or that of our loved ones, because we are readily taught how to address it. From a young age, we learn to clean wounds, take medication, and seek medical help for physical ailments. However, such readiness and education are almost entirely absent when it comes to mental pain. Second, the mere fact that someone would choose bodily pain over mental distress reveals the immense weight of mental suffering, a burden often unseen but profoundly felt.

Mental pain can arise from mental health struggles or even physical health challenges that lead to emotional distress. Kabir recounts the story of a classmate, Nandini, whose family endured unimaginable hardships. Nandini's sister and mother were diagnosed as HIV-positive years ago. Because of the deep-rooted stigma surrounding the illness, they were shunned by their extended family and ostracised by their community. Even Kabir was discouraged from associating with Nandini. Eventually, societal pressure forced Nandini to drop out of school, plunging her into an overwhelming state of despair.

What makes Nandini's story especially poignant is what happened afterwards. Over time, with medical help and persistent effort, her family regained their physical health. They managed to mitigate the virus's effects and build a relatively normal life, at least in terms of their physical well-being. Nevertheless, the stigma remained.

The community's rejection lingered like an unhealed wound, isolating them socially. Tragically, they began to internalise this rejection, convincing themselves that they were unworthy of acceptance.

This phenomenon is heartbreakingly familiar. When the majority clings to a misinformed belief, the marginalised minority often starts to believe it too, absorbing the prejudice into their own identity. It is reminiscent of the fable of the tree that withers and dies, not because it lacked sunlight or water, but because it was subjected to relentless scorn. Words, perceptions, and stigma have the power to wound in ways that no physical ailment ever could.

Ultimately, after battling the illness for three to four long years, Nandini's sister could no longer endure the crushing weight of societal marginalisation and the relentless stares that seemed to whisper, *something is wrong with you*. One day, she attempted to take her own life. Thankfully, her attempt was not successful, but the scars of that day remain etched in Nandini's memory. She often reflects with a quiet pain, saying, *"The mental distress caused by the stigma could have killed my sister faster and more brutally than the illness ever could."*

This is the heartbreaking truth. In the absence of emotional or mental support, even the strongest of souls can begin to crumble. In the face of physical illness, people are often quick to offer comfort and solidarity, holding hands, sending meals, or simply being present. However, even this support has its limits when it comes to stigmatised conditions like HIV. With mental illness, however, such compassion becomes a distant dream. The silence is deafening.

Kabir believes this lack of visibility is at the heart of another reason why people resort to self-harm: to make their pain seen. A wound on the arm becomes a tangible cry for help, saying, *"Look, this cut hurts, and I carry the same kind of wounds in my mind. You cannot see them, but they are just as real, and they hurt no less."*

This raw need to be acknowledged, to have the invisible made visible, is a profound reminder of how desperately people yearn for understanding. It is not just about the physical pain; it is about being heard, seen, and validated in a world that too often turns away from what it cannot immediately comprehend.

It is easy to dismiss people with mental health issues as attention seekers. However, even if they are seeking attention, is that inherently wrong? Isn't it a sign that someone yearns to be heard, seen, and acknowledged? Tragically, some people find that they are only noticed when life and death are at stake. This lack of recognition drives them to extremes, leading them to make unhealthy decisions in their desperation to be seen.

For some, self-harm becomes a way to make their invisible pain visible, a plea for care and understanding. The irony, however, is stark. Kabir, for instance, used to hide his wounds. He was not comfortable with others seeing them because he knew they would not try to understand his pain. Instead, he feared being labelled, judged, or dismissed. Moreover, even when someone did show concern for his wounds, it rarely extended beyond the physical injury. No one honestly tried to grasp the pain that caused it.

This highlights a troubling truth: the kind of support many claim to offer, especially those who consider themselves progressive about mental health, often remains superficial. They may tend to the physical injury caused by self-harm, but they frequently fail to acknowledge or address the more profound emotional distress behind it. Stopping self-harm is just the first step.

Even mental health professionals are trained to prioritise immediate physical injuries before addressing the psychological root of the issue. The crucial difference is that professionals are required to take that next step and delve into the mental and emotional causes. As loved ones, our role should not end with physical first aid either. We, too, must provide what can be called psychological first aid. Simply bandaging a wound is not enough when that wound is merely a symptom of much deeper mental pain.

Sadly, mental pain often requires more support than physical pain, and it is here that we frequently falter. This lack of adequate care pushes people who self-harm into a relentless cycle: harm themselves, heal, and then repeat. The underlying issue, the root cause of their pain, remains unaddressed, leaving them trapped in this spiral.

Kabir recognised this gap and was determined to make a difference. He enrolled in a course on psychological first aid, where he learned the importance of being present for someone in distress. The training emphasised tending to physical wounds first, if necessary, but also stressed that proper care does not stop there. Mental support is equally crucial, and often, it is the part that matters most.

An essential insight Kabir gained from this course was that mental distress may or may not follow a visible physical situation, but mental health issues are physical in themselves. Depression, anxiety, OCD, and schizophrenia are not abstract states of mind; they are rooted in the physical functioning of the brain. The brain is an organ, like the heart or lungs. When it does not secrete certain chemicals as it should, it is a physical issue. The challenge is that the consequences of this dysfunction are not always visible. Unlike a broken bone or a bleeding wound, mental illness hides in plain sight, making it harder to understand and easier to overlook.

7 Depression

Depression, also known as major depressive disorder, is a prevalent and severe mental health condition. American Psychiatric Association. (2022) defines it as "a mood disorder that adversely impacts a person's feelings, thoughts, actions, and perception of the world". Beck et al. (1979) frame it as "a state marked by enduring negative views of oneself, the world, and the future". Depression consists of several building blocks: loss of interest or pleasure, a state of mind that exists over a period of time dealing with this crisis, accompanied by other symptoms, and results in distress or disability. It is not merely prolonged sadness but a complex disorder involving emotional, cognitive, and physiological changes that can severely disrupt daily life and overall well-being. Due to its effects on thinking and emotional regulation, depression is a major risk factor for suicidal thoughts and behaviours.

People with depression might seem withdrawn or sometimes visibly upset. Their thoughts are often negative. They feel they are hopeless and have the idea in their mind that things will never improve. Feelings of worthlessness, excessive guilt, and self-criticism are common, along with persistent rumination over past failures and events. Energy levels tend to be low, making even simple tasks tiring. Motivation and focus may be reduced, and they might find it hard to socialise or handle daily tasks. In severe cases, depression can lead to thoughts of death or suicide, especially when the person feels stuck in their pain and unable to see any way out.

From a suicide gatekeeper's perspective, supporting someone with depression demands patience, consistency, and emotional sensitivity. Responses from the people in crisis are often slow, and improvements tend to occur gradually; rushing or expecting quick changes can add pressure and increase feelings of inadequacy.

An important element in dealing with people who are depressed is taking their concerns seriously while listening to them with empathy. Paying attention to sudden mood shifts is equally important. Even a mood swing from being very sad to being happy and full of humour. A clear example can be found in the movie The Joker (2019): *"The worst part of having a mental illness is people expect you to behave as if you do not"*. This sometimes may indicate a decision to attempt suicide rather than true recovery. So it is necessary to guide people with depression and tell them there is hope. Supporting them in finding sources of hope, exploring the options, and offering positive alternatives without ignoring their mental pain. Occasionally, it might be useful to repeat the information, as their window of tolerance is small, while still giving them all the room to express themselves.

7.1 A story: Everybody hurts

Chuck has been navigating the turbulent waters of mental health for a long time. His journey, like so many others, has been anything but linear. There have been moments of hope and progress, followed by setbacks that pulled him back into the depths. Along the way, he has lost people, connections severed by the weight of his struggles, as often happens with those battling mental illness.

Chuck believes, and rightly so, that mental illness is a disability. It is not something that can be willed away or ignored; it has a profound, often invisible grip on one's life. At times, it has robbed him of the ability to perform even the simplest daily tasks. There were mornings when just getting out of bed felt impossible, not because of any physical ailment, but because of an unseen weight pressing down on him. This weight shifted with time. Some days, it was crushing, almost unbearable. Other days, it eased, becoming just heavy enough to be endured. On rare occasions, it felt as light as a feather, allowing him a fleeting sense of relief.

In a recent conversation, Chuck shared something deeply personal with me. He recounted how people often told him that his struggles were "all in his head." They claimed that by simply thinking more positively, he could overcome his pain in no time. However, Chuck did not choose this path, nor does he find any joy in it. "If I could flip a switch and feel better, I would," he said, his voice a mix of frustration and sadness.

His emotions swing like a pendulum. When he is happy, he feels an unparalleled sense of joy, as though he is standing on top of the world. But when sadness engulfs him, it is devastating, an abyss he struggles to climb out of. His psychiatrist is currently exploring a possible diagnosis of Bipolar Disorder (BPD). While nothing is certain yet, one thing is clear: Chuck's mind does not bend to his will. He cannot force it into submission, cannot simply think his way out of his reality.

Chuck asked me a question that lingered in my mind long after our conversation. "Is the brain not part of the body?" he began, his voice heavy with frustration. "When I have physical issues, I am treated, taken to a doctor, and cared for. Nevertheless, when it comes to my mental health, I am just told to 'think positively' and expected to feel better magically. I am so tired of this. It makes me angry at my loved ones who do not try to understand. Isn't it their responsibility, as the people who love me, to at least attempt to grasp the concept of mental illness so they can support me better?"

The pain in his words was palpable, but what he shared next was even more haunting. "I have always wanted to die," he admitted, his tone raw with honesty. "The idea of disappearing has always seemed so... fascinating. Not having to deal with this invisible weight anymore. But now I am scared to die. Not because I suddenly want to live, but because I am terrified of being forgotten by the people I love.

"It is strange, isn't it? On one hand, it feels like a blessing that they might move on quickly, that my absence would not cause them prolonged pain. However, on the other hand, it hurts. It hurts to realise how immaterial I have become in the lives of the people I love so deeply. I might exist in their memories, but if I were gone, they would not even notice for a long time. They have already distanced themselves from me, likely because being close to someone so consumed by depression is not easy. I cannot blame them for that. Nevertheless, it is scary to think my death would not matter any more than my life seems to."

He paused, his voice trembling slightly as he continued. "In a way, it is good. Fewer people would be hurt by my absence. However, it leaves me feeling more alone than ever. My parents are the exception; they would be devastated. I am alive because of them. They love me too much for me to inflict that kind of pain on them. However, it feels unfair, doesn't it? The only reason I am still here is that I have this anchor, one that exists because of obligation, not choice.

"Then again, I am reminded that not everyone has this kind of anchor. It is a privilege in its own way. It is a good reason not to die, I suppose. However, it also makes dying easier to contemplate. If my absence would not cause much pain to others, why should I keep enduring mine? Maybe stopping to exist would be the simplest way to end it all." Chuck's words carried the weight of a soul stretched thin between love and despair, hope and resignation. It was a painful reminder of how vital understanding and connection are, and how devastating their absence can be for someone already battling the darkest corners of their mind.

"By distancing themselves from me when all I needed was for them to simply be there, not even to help, just to not abandon me actively, aren't they sending a message? A signal that the world is better off without me? That their lives are happier, more peaceful, and more content in my absence?"

8 Mental illness

Mental illness, according to the American Psychiatric Association (2022), refers to "a broad range of mental health conditions, also called mental disorders, that affect an individual's mood, thinking, perception, behaviour, and ability to function in daily life". These mental health conditions can influence how people relate to others, manage stress, make decisions, and regulate emotions. There is a variety of mental illnesses, including depression, anxiety disorders, schizophrenia, eating disorders, and addictive behaviours. The spectrum is actually far wider and varies in severity, duration, and impact, according to the World Health Organisation (2023).

Mental illnesses are not the result of a single cause. Turecki et al. (2019) state that they result from complex interactions among biological, psychological, and social factors throughout a person's life. The development or intensity of the mental health conditions can also be influenced by neurobiological differences, early life experiences, trauma, chronic stress, and social conditions. As a result, mental illness should be understood as a health condition rather than a personal weakness or moral failing.

One commonly observed feature of mental illness is difficulty concentrating or focusing. Individuals may feel disconnected from reality, struggle to complete tasks, or experience racing or fragmented thoughts. Rock et al. (2014) found that the issues around attention and focus are particularly common in conditions such as depression, anxiety disorders, and attention-related disorders. What happens is that the cognitive resources are often taken over by intrusive thoughts or emotional distress.

One of the other signs which happens frequently is persistent or constant anxiety, characterised by fear or worry that feels excessive, uncontrollable, or disproportionate to the actual situation. Anxiety can place the body in a prolonged state of physiological arousal, activating stress responses that interfere with sleep, digestion, and emotional regulation. Craske et al. (2017) suggest that if anxiety becomes chronic, it can significantly impair quality of life and increase vulnerability to other mental health difficulties.

Mood changes are also central to many mental illnesses. These may involve prolonged sadness, emotional numbness, irritability, or rapid mood fluctuations that can occur from day to day or even hour to hour. The American Psychiatric Association (2022) points out that mood disturbances are a defining feature of depressive and bipolar disorders, but they also occur in trauma-related and anxiety disorders. Such changes often affect motivation, self-esteem, and interpersonal relationships.

Mental illness frequently affects social functioning, leading to social withdrawal. People may isolate themselves from family, friends, or colleagues. The more they withdraw, the harder it is to make contact and help them.

8.1 A story: Feel the pain

Mental illnesses creep in unnoticed; they are insidious, the weight growing heavier over time. One feature is that they remain under the surface. One cannot compare it to a wound that bleeds and demands care and attention. They neither mark the body with visible signs of pain or distress, nor start with a whisper and then a scream. It begins very subtly, like a strange sensation of numbness in the leg. It is perhaps nothing at first, just a fleeting discomfort. One convinces oneself to keep running. It is fine. It must be in one's head, and so one runs until, one day, one's legs collapse and give up. The pain is excruciating, but there is no visible wound. People around them watch, confusion in their eyes. In their mind, they ask themselves what has happened or what could be wrong with this person. This is how cruel mental illness can be. It reveals itself late and often in ways that, in the long run, are impossible to ignore. They manifest like a breakdown in the middle of a conversation, tears that fall far too often, silence too heavy to be mere exhaustion. Yet it is easier to dismiss mental illness by calling it attention-seeking behaviour, by insisting that it is all in the mind until it becomes too persistent, too raw, and too uncomfortable to witness.

If left untreated or unacknowledged, the illness and its weight only grow. They will not go unnoticed forever. Mental illnesses twist and manifest in ways that frighten both the sufferer and the people around them. The longer help is not available, the more painful it becomes for the sufferer. When a mind is drowning in negative emotions and goes through dark thoughts, it does not go quietly beneath the surface. At that point, the mind wants to acknowledge that suffering is taking place and asks for support from another person.

Haley remembers reading an article in the newspaper about how a caretaker can stay steady while supporting a loved one in pain. It is very important to remain grounded, not to be pulled under, but it is equally vital to understand, as a caretaker, what truly helps and what only prolongs the struggle. To use a metaphor, it is like reaching out to a friend who is drowning in the ocean. Our first instinct is to save them, to grasp their hand before the waves get them. But what if you do not know the depth of the water? What if the current is too dangerous, or sharks swim in the dark below? What if, in desperation to pull them up, you sink alongside them? Blaming a person for not getting better despite all well-intentioned efforts is equivalent to blaming a drowning person for pulling you under when you were the one who jumped into the water without knowing how to save them.

As Haley reads the article, she realises something. Even though caregivers deserve rest and compassion, they also bear the responsibility of learning, equally, if not more so. The article speaks about how caring for someone with deep depression can take a toll on the caregiver, how their pain ripples outward and pierces those who love them. And this is true. But there is another truth just as important: helping a loved one was never meant to be comfortable. Healing is not like a gentle tide that sways you softly; it is like being caught in a stormy sea. If you choose to stand beside the suffering, you must learn not only how to handle the waves, but how to understand them. This is not to say that helping a loved one is meant to be traumatising. It is not. Self-awareness and balance can keep one from losing oneself entirely. However, comfort was never part of the deal. Supporting a person with a mental illness is not easy, not gentle, and certainly not wrapped in warmth. Most of the time, it is raw, painful, and often exhausting. People with mental illness are often called violent, aggressive, and unpredictable. But what people in general do not see is that most of the anger is turned inward, eating them alive. From the outside, it is often seen as frustration, outbursts, or reckless desperation, which is only the tip of the iceberg, the rest of which is often overlooked. Acts of aggression and chaos should never be used as an excuse, but neither are they to be dismissed as the traits of a violent, attention-seeking person. People have to look at and treat this as wounds, not as weapons. Haley has carried her illness for so long that she cannot remember a time when she was not under its weight. She has seen friendships and relationships slip through her fingers like sand. Most of them fell apart when her illness was growing and becoming more visible. It resulted in self-harm, suicide attempts, and the kind of pain that makes people look away because it is uncomfortable to witness. It is human to need space, to step back and breathe. Equally important is it as a human to stay, to hold on even when it is messy, even when it is painful, because love cannot be measured by how easily things shine when they are new, but by how fiercely we choose to love when they are old and faded.

People often miss one's cry for help because it is usually whispered, at least at first. Questions go around, such as: *"She seemed so happy, what could have gone wrong? She barely complained, so why would she harm herself?"* And when the cries are no longer subtle, when they turn raw and desperate, we turn away. The message people give to those who suffer is: *"I am a good friend, but your pain is too loud, too messy, too much. I cannot bear to watch."* It makes no sense. Mental illnesses go unnoticed until they become unbearable, until they soar beyond control. By the time they are visible, they are already too much, too heavy, too complicated to be easily mended. Is there, then, an optimum stage of suffering? A precise level of despair one must reach to be deemed worthy of help, bad enough to need saving, but not so bad that it makes others uncomfortable? No attempt to die, but a few scars on your skin. The message is then: *"Break, but break quietly. Shatter, but keep it neat and tidy"* as if pain follows a rulebook. As if suffering should be polite. Mental illnesses are not just quiet tears behind closed doors. They include emotions magnified and distorted by the weight of suffering. They include incessant crying, anger that boils too fast, words that cut too deep, and fights that flare into something ugly. But these are still cries for help. There is no volume button; pain cannot be adjusted to a level that feels comfortable to those around it. Mental illnesses are ugly, and this is the truth.

They are often bearable to loved ones as long as they can be masked. As long as they are not visible to the outside world. Keeping up the image that everything is okay. Just as long as people can smile through the pain and function as if nothing is wrong. The moment cracks show, the moment the cries become too much, self-harm too visible, desperation too raw, people step away. As if saying: I will help you as long as your wounds are just deep enough to sting, but not so deep that you are unable to keep pretending you are fine. Suffering is painful, and pain does not ask for permission before it is seen. As people, we do not get to choose how pretty someone's struggles should be before they deserve help. People need to respond to the cry for humanity.

9 Trauma

Trauma is defined by the American Psychological Association (2022) as: "An emotional response to a terrible event like an accident, rape, or natural disaster. Immediately after the event, shock and denial are typical. Longer-term reactions include unpredictable emotions, flashbacks, strained relationships, and even physical symptoms like headaches or nausea".

Maté (2023) offers a slightly different definition: "trauma is not what happens to a person, but what happens within them. In line with its Greek origins, trauma means a wound: an unhealed one, and one the person is compelled to defend against by means of constricting their own ability to feel, to be present, to respond flexibly to situations."

Trauma influences our lives in many deep ways that are often misunderstood. Sometimes, when behaviours are judged without understanding their origins, it can feel unfair. Note that people do not merely react to what is happening now; they respond to how they perceive it, a key idea in trauma research. Van der Kolk (2014) found that the nervous system tends to respond more to perceived threats than to actual events. Because of this, we often respond not to the present moment but to past experiences stored in our bodies and emotions, shaping how we react today through memories we might not even be aware of (Ogden, Minton, and Pain, 2006).

It is important to understand that under the surface, a person who has experienced trauma is still fundamentally healthy. Trauma does not wipe out who you are at your core; instead, it hides it behind protective adaptations, as Herman (1992) stated. That is why it is so helpful to see people as whole humans, not just problems, and why trauma-informed care focuses on understanding behaviour as a form of communication rather than something wrong or broken. When caring for others, asking questions like "What happened to you?" rather than "What is wrong with you?" helps reframe symptoms as responses to overwhelming experiences (Harris & Fallot, 2001).

Trauma can often lead us to develop long-term survival strategies. While these strategies were essential at one point, they can become limiting later in life. For example, emotional numbing or suppression might have helped someone survive when escape or support were unavailable (van der Kolk, 2014). Over time, this can cause us to ignore our feelings to get through the day, leading to a sense of disconnection from ourselves. We might lose touch with our bodily sensations, our emotions, or even our sense of who we are (Ogden et al., 2006). When addictive behaviours appear, it is helpful to look beyond the addiction itself to understand the deep pain behind it. Addiction often is an effort to manage unbearable internal states, not a reflection of moral failure (Maté, 2008).

Childhood trauma is especially impactful because young brains rely so heavily on safe, caring relationships to develop healthily. Children are not hurt just by the pain itself but because they are left alone with that pain. That underlines the importance of caring; parents, family members or caregivers who can help buffer stress (Herman, 1992). For healthy growth, children need secure, genuine connections where emotions can be experienced and managed safely within relationships, Bowlby (1988) says. When such attachment is missing, the child's nervous system adapts to constant threat, shaping long-term coping strategies and how they see themselves.

As trauma carries into adulthood, it often shows up in behaviours, relationships, and how well we can regulate ourselves. Life might feel like a rerun of old wounds. The nervous system can get used to chaos, van der Kolk (2014) found. A sign is that chaos will feel familiar and safer than calm. Experiences like verbal and emotional abuse can condition someone toward self-destruction and self-sabotage. They can lead to feelings of worthlessness and danger that stick deep inside (Herman, 1992). Coping mechanisms like addiction and dissociation might serve as temporary relief but can also create and deepen feelings of disconnection, Maté (2008) said. Many survivors of childhood abuse also face thoughts of suicide, which is sadly common with a history of adverse childhood experiences. Felitti et al. (1998) show that there is a clear link between these early experiences and increased suicide risk. Internally, various parts of ourselves sometimes seem out of sync with our adult selves, reflecting the fragmentation and adaptive dissociation that developed in response to overwhelming experiences (Schwartz, 1995).

Trauma can arise through three forms of exposure, each affecting people in different but significant ways, namely direct, secondary and vicarious trauma. Direct trauma occurs when a person is personally exposed to situations which involve serious risk or harm, such as victimisation, such as rape or bullying, natural disasters, or war. It often leaves lasting psychological and emotional impacts. A secondary trauma, also known as compassion fatigue, develops through continued, frequent, or close contact with people who have experienced direct trauma, as caregivers, professionals, or loved ones. The people who help the people with the direct trauma may absorb emotional distress over time. Vicarious trauma is caused by indirect exposure to traumatic events through reports, descriptions, or graphic footage, where repeated engagement with horrific material can alter one's emotional well-being, perceptions of safety, and worldview, even without direct involvement.

Trauma is not who a person is; it is what happened and how they survived it. Such an event happened suddenly and unexpectedly. This will give people a sense of unpredictability and a lack of control. Healing becomes possible only when safety, connection, and understanding replace judgment. This will allow the healthy person beneath the trauma to re-emerge.

9.1 Trauma and the brain

Trauma can significantly alter how key brain systems function, helping explain many of the symptoms people experience after a traumatic event, such as intrusive memories, hypervigilance, and emotional ups and downs. The amygdala, part of the brain's threat-detection system, detects danger and triggers a fight-or-flight response. After trauma, the amygdala can become overactive, responding not only to actual threats but also to reminders or memories of past dangers, even when no real danger is present. This heightened reactivity can lead to intense emotional reactions and a constant feeling of being on edge. At the same time, the hippocampus, which usually helps us store memories with precise details about when and where things happened, does not function as well under ongoing stress. When trauma interferes with hippocampal functioning, memories may not be properly labelled, so past events can feel as if they are happening all over again. Trauma can also reduce activity in the prefrontal cortex. Some of the functions of the prefrontal cortex are decision-making, focusing, and emotion regulation, which can make it harder to plan, concentrate, and keep emotions in check. Together, these changes in the brain help explain why intrusive thoughts, memory issues, and negative feelings are common features of traumatic stress.

And the memories can be understood as films that play in our minds, where, under normal circumstances, we have control over which ones we watch and when they begin or end. After experiencing trauma, however, some of these films become difficult or distressing to view, and we may try hard to avoid them. In the situation of post-traumatic stress disorder (PTSD), it can feel as though a rogue projectionist has taken control of the projector, forcing certain films to play without our consent and at unexpected times. Having no control over those films can be deeply upsetting. This often leads to people trying to push away their painful memories even more, despite how persistent and intrusive they may become.

9.2 Traumatic stress and its psychological impact

Traumatic stress is defined by the American Psychiatric Association (2022) as: *"the psychological and physiological response that occurs following exposure to a traumatic event, such as serious injury, violence, disaster, or threat to life."* While many individuals experience temporary distress after trauma, some develop persistent symptoms that significantly impair daily functioning. When these symptoms endure, they may meet criteria for trauma-related disorders such as Post-Traumatic Stress Disorder.

Another definition, by Mitchell and Everly (1996), is:"Any event which has sufficient emotional power to overwhelm a person's ability to cope."

Traumatic stress reactions are commonly organised into symptom clusters, including intrusive symptoms and negative alterations in cognition and mood, both of which reflect disruptions in memory processing, emotional regulation, and meaning-making according to Brewin et al. (2010).

Trauma symptoms: intrusive moments

Intrusive symptoms involve involuntary and distressing re-experiencing of the traumatic event. These symptoms reflect difficulties in integrating the traumatic memory into autobiographical memory and are a hallmark of traumatic stress disorders (Ehlers & Clark, 2000).

Trauma symptoms – intrusive moments include:

- Recurrent, unwanted distressing memories of the traumatic event
- Reliving the traumatic event as if it were happening again (flashbacks)

- Upsetting dreams or nightmares about the traumatic event
- Severe emotional distress or physical reactions to something that reminds you of the traumatic event

These intrusive experiences are often triggered by reminders (internal or external) that resemble aspects of the trauma and can provoke intense fear, panic, or physiological arousal, even in objectively safe environments (van der Kolk, 2014).

Negative cognitions and mood

Negative changes in cognition and mood, which can be noticed in people's beliefs and values, emotional responsiveness, and interpersonal functioning, are another characteristic of traumatic stress. Janof-Bulman (1992) noticed that trauma can fundamentally disrupt an individual's assumptions about safety, trust, and control, leading to persistent negative appraisals of oneself and the world.

Negative cognitions/mood symptoms include:

- Negative thoughts about yourself, other people, or the world
- Hopelessness about the future
- Memory problems, including not remembering important aspects of the traumatic event
- Difficulty maintaining close relationships
- Feeling detached from family and friends
- Lack of interest in activities you once enjoyed
- Difficulty experiencing positive emotions
- Feeling emotionally numb

All of the symptoms mentioned above are closely linked to avoidance, emotional numbing, and depressive features. The symptoms also often contribute to long-term functional impairment if left untreated, according to the American Psychiatric Association (2022).

Clinical and social implications

Traumatic stress affects not only internal emotional experiences. It also affects social functioning. Herman (1992) states that emotional numbing and detachment can interfere with intimacy and support-seeking, which are otherwise protective factors in recovery. If we identify this early and intervene with the help of professionals, it can help to reduce symptom severity and improve quality of life (Lewis et al., 2020).

Traumatic stress reactions often organise into different symptom clusters, such as intrusive symptoms and negative changes in thoughts and mood. These reflect disruptions in how memories are processed, emotional responses are regulated, and experiences are given meaning (Brewin et al., 2010).

9.3 A Story: Lose yourself

Rahul is an athlete, a dreamer with a fire that never dims. His ambition is vast, his determination unshakable. People admire his strength and stamina. The press even calls him one of the best in his field. Today, Rahul is standing at the starting line of an 800-meter race. His heart is pounding with excitement. He can not wait to run and go for glory. The gunshot sounds through the air, and the race begins. Ten athletes in this competition surge forward, feet pounding against the track at full speed. Rahul runs with everything he has, his mind focused, his heart set on victory. Each step is a testament to his dedication, his dreams.

But soon, Rahul begins to struggle. His breaths grow heavy, his legs protest with every step. He pushes on, refusing to quit. And then, he stumbles. The crowd gasps. Before he can steady himself, he falls.

A wave of murmurs goes through the stands. The crowd even started to make fun of him.

"What is wrong with him? He cannot even manage 800 meters!"

"Everyone else is doing just fine, why cannot he keep up?"

The words cut deep, piercing Rahul's already fragile determination to win the race. He feels the weight of their judgment pressing down on him. Perhaps they are right, he thinks. Maybe he does not belong here. Maybe it is best to give up.

But there is something the crowd already knows, something that has not been told you yet: Rahul has only one working leg. He is the only disabled athlete in the race.

Now, knowing this, let us revisit the scene. Imagine the crowd watching as Rahul falls, understanding the extraordinary effort it took for him to even be on that track. Would they still have ridiculed him? Alternatively, would there be a different response of the crowd, raising their voices in support, cheering him on, saying, *"Look at him go! Despite everything, he has been pushing forward. He is the real champion today."*

Perspective changes everything. When people see the hurdles someone else faces, their judgment often gives way to admiration. Effort becomes the victory, and resilience becomes the story worth celebrating.

Well, this did not actually happen. In reality, we have separate teams for disabled and non-disabled athletes. If Rahul had participated in a race alongside athletes with fully functioning legs and had fallen or decided to give up, the reaction would have been entirely different. The crowd would not have booed him. They would have recognised the immense challenge he faced, running the same race as those without his limitations. Instead of judgment, there would have been empathy. Instead of ridicule, there would have been admiration.

No one would have said, *"Everyone else managed to cover the distance; what is wrong with him?" People's voices would rise in support instead, saying, "Look at Rahul! Despite everything, he gave it his all. For that, he is the true winner because he did not give up."* The difference in this lies in understanding. When people acknowledge the unique struggles a person faces, their perception shifts. The effort a person has put in becomes more important than results, and perseverance becomes the ultimate triumph, as you often see in the Olympic Games.

Life itself is a race, and we are all participants. The difference between someone with a healthy brain and someone battling mental illness is no different from the contrast between Rahul and the other athletes.

The irony, though, is stark; we cannot have two separate races in life, as we do in the Olympics and Paralympics. Life does not divide its challenges into categories for those with healthy minds and those fighting internal battles.

Nevertheless, is not unity in diversity something we believe in? Should not that belief extend to embracing both individuals with no mental illness and those who live with it?

This is the story of Rahul. He is not an athlete. He has both legs working, and he has never participated in a sports event. However, he is a player in the game of life, a game where his opponent is a severe and recurring mental health condition. Every day is a competition, and every moment is a challenge.

Rahul struggles to navigate life's course. Tasks that his peers accomplish with ease take him longer, require more effort, and demand immeasurable patience. Sometimes, he feels like giving up halfway, the weight of it all too much to bear.

And then come the remarks: *"Everyone has issues, but they are still managing."*

Yes, everyone has issues. But not everyone has a mental illness. The truth is, living with a mental illness is like running a race with invisible weights strapped to your body, while everyone else sprints unencumbered. It is exhausting, isolating, and often misunderstood.

In today's world, if one were to visit a mental health professional, the chances are high that many of us would receive a diagnosis of some mental health condition. The severity may vary, but the struggles are undeniable. Those who are diagnosed gain an awareness of their battles, while those who remain undiagnosed often continue without understanding the weight they carry.

Rahul sometimes wonders if ignorance is truly bliss. Before his diagnosis, he pushed himself relentlessly to feel better. He believed that sheer effort could chase away the heaviness he felt inside. However, now, with a diagnosis in hand, Rahul knows better. He understands that forcing himself to feel happy is the right thing to do. It is even counterproductive in the long run. Being aware of that has given him clarity, while also laying bare the complexity of his journey.

While his peers, unburdened by diagnosed mental health challenges, navigate life with relative ease, Rahul spends his days and resources on doctors, therapy, exercises, and journaling. He invests so much to catch a glimpse of the ease they seem to experience effortlessly.

This is the truth of living with mental illness. Given the same problem, a person with a mental illness needs more patience, more care, and more support to navigate through it than someone with optimal mental health.

Rahul often says, "People less mentally ill than I am are privileged. To them, I am toxic." Moreover, in many ways, that is true. There is a vast gap between those who have mental health struggles and those who do not, and that gap needs to be bridged. This divide mirrors the social separation between the 'haves' and the 'have-nots,' except the resource in question here is good mental health.

People like Rahul are a minority, largely because not everyone is diagnosed or even aware of the mental health issues they face. Shouldn't it make sense that, despite the differences, they have to run the same race as the privileged ones, with their superior resources and advantages? Moreover, when they falter, when they cannot keep going, they are met with rebuke, criticism, and misunderstanding.

Unfortunately, neither the race nor the rules can be changed. Nevertheless, our attitude toward those running it, especially those struggling, can.

To give another example, imagine playing Jenga. Ritu has a full set of pieces, a complete, stable tower that she can build upon. Rahul, however, has a set with fewer pieces, a tower that is inherently less stable. To reach the same height as Ritu's tower, Rahul has to adjust, leaving gaps and placing pieces carefully, knowing the structure is not as solid.

When the game begins, Ritu may pull 5 to 10 pieces from her tower without causing any real harm to the structure. However, Rahul's tower, weakened by fewer pieces, is likely to collapse with the same moves. The difference is clear: the foundation for Rahul is fragile, not because he is playing any less skilfully, but because he is working with fewer resources.

This is the truth for people like Rahul. They do not have the luxury of a full set of pieces, whether it is mental strength, stability, or resources, and they have to play the game against those who do. It would not make sense to ask, "If Ritu can do it, why cannot Rahul?" When it comes to mental health, the difference is often invisible, and it is easy to forget that some people are carrying a far heavier load than others.

Rahul is playing with one leg. It sometimes feels to him like a bag of stones strapped to his back, while others run with ease. So, when he stumbles, breaks down, or gives up earlier than others, it is not because he is weak or does not try hard enough. It is simply the reality of the game he is forced to play, one with fewer pieces, less stability, and more challenges to overcome.

10 Learned helplessness

Learned helplessness is a psychological condition in which someone may feel they cannot influence or change their situation, even when opportunities for improvement exist. Seligman and Maier (1967) found that when people are repeatedly exposed to situations they cannot control and that are unpleasant, they often stop trying to escape or improve them. Over time, this belief becomes part of how they see the world, affecting how they face challenges and opportunities.

Usually, learned helplessness develops after experiencing mental trauma, abuse, or psychological harm repeatedly. When efforts to resist or improve conditions keep failing or are met with punishment, the person might start to expect that all future efforts will also fail as a self-fulfilling prophecy. This can lead to feelings of powerlessness and a sense of incapability. Even when circumstances change or help becomes available, people might not notice or trust these new opportunities. Their inner thoughts might shift from an initial *"I cannot do this right now"* to a *"There is nothing I can do"* attitude, which encourages passivity and withdrawal.

The emotional and behavioural effects of learned helplessness can be deeply impactful. People might stop standing up for themselves, avoid solving problems, and withdraw from social interactions, often suffering quietly. What is very common is that feelings of hopelessness, low motivation, and reduced self-esteem, and these feelings can leave a lasting psychological effect. In mental health and suicide prevention, learned helplessness is especially concerning because it can lead people to believe that their pain is unavoidable and that there are no options left. Understanding this condition is particularly important for caregivers, mental health professionals, and supporters, because helping someone regain a sense of control, choice, and agency is a vital step toward healing and recovery. Learned helplessness is not a permanent trait or personal failure. Instead, it is a learned response to uncontrollable conditions and can be unlearned. With appropriate support, individuals can rebuild confidence, reengage with challenges, and regain a sense of meaning, choice, and personal power.

10.1 A story: Lean on me

Rhea was struggling with something in her brain. She was walking down a road where sunlight and storm clouds often traded places without, it seemed, any warning. At times, she felt grounded, even joyful. However, at other times, it felt different. It was as if Rhea were weighed down by an invisible heaviness in her brain, making even breathing a task. Her journey so far with depression had been unpredictable, unrelenting, though sometimes, very rarely, gentle.

All along, there had been a friend, Eric. He was her mentor and steady anchor. He was the kind of person who never tried to fix things for her, but knew exactly when to listen, when to nudge, and when to stay.

On a particular day, Eric shared a very simple picture with her. It was an image divided into four coloured zones: green, yellow, orange, and red. Each colour represented a state of mind, from ready and balanced to reacting and injured to critically unwell, the point where one needs intense care. It was called the mental health continuum. Very soon, it became more than just a chart; it became a language of expression for her. Every time she talked to Eric, he began with a gentle check-in: "Hey Rhea, what colour are you at today?"

It had become a ritual. In that question of Eric's, there lay both curiosity and care. Furthermore, this curiosity was not a formality, but an invitation; an opening to speak about what bothered Rhea at times.

Rhea felt less need to wrestle with words to explain her feelings. She did not have to say: "I feel on edge today, and I might snap if one more thing goes wrong." Instead, she could say: "I am a bit yellow today, I think." When she was doing well, she did not need to overexplain her joy. She could say, "I am green today," smiling, because that single word captured all the joy, confidence, and calm she felt in that moment.

Eric also celebrated her greens and sometimes her transitions from red or orange to yellow. It was not done with hollow encouragement, but with genuine warmth. In this way, it would always remind her how far she had come. Moreover, on days when she would slip back to orange or red, Eric did not panic. He would listen, asking her questions. Determined, he helped her find the energy to try moving towards green again.

It also helped Rhea explain how she was feeling without having to dive into the details of her life. It prevented her from giving too much information, making things uncomfortable, yet it still put her state of mind across very clearly.

She thought this colour code had helped her do more than communicate. It had helped her understand herself. Recognising the shades of her own emotions allowed her to understand the depth of help she needed or could provide to herself. There was no fixed amount of care that fit every colour. It was a gradient, where colours sometimes blended, sometimes shifted, and so did the requirement for help and the time needed for healing.

It also carried a powerful message. One does not have to wait for someone to turn red to offer help. A kind word at yellow or orange can prevent a descent into darker shades. Similarly, it is equally important to acknowledge someone's green: their good days. It helps them stay there longer.

Help is not supposed to be a last resort. It is supposed to be a way of living. It is like the sunlight we provide to each other, so that we can all be green, or at least yellow, or at least walking toward green again.

11 Bullying and suicide: understanding the connection

Bullying is not a harmless rite of passage. For many children and adolescents, it is a deeply distressing experience that can leave lasting emotional, psychological, and social scars. Being bullied can significantly trigger suicidal thoughts and behaviours, especially when bullying is combined with other vulnerabilities. Understanding this relationship is essential for prevention, early intervention, and effective support.

Bullying is defined by Volk et al. (2014) as: “Aggressive, goal-directed behaviour that occurs in the context of a power imbalance and causes harm to another individual”.

There are four characteristics. Firstly, it is an intentional and harmful behaviour. Secondly, it involves a power imbalance, where the person being bullied has less social, physical, or psychological power than the person or persons bullying. Thirdly, it is often used to gain or maintain status or dominance, or to get something, so it is strategic or goal-oriented. Lastly, for something to be called bullying, repetition is not required, even though it happens repeatedly.

Both children and adolescents who are bullied often experience a wide range of negative effects that can continue well beyond the bullying itself. Emotionally, bullying is strongly linked to depression and anxiety, as well as changes in sleep and eating patterns and a loss of interest in activities that once brought joy or a sense of belonging. Over time, repeated humiliation or being the target can destroy self-esteem. This can lead to deep feelings of shame that affect how young people see themselves and their place in the world.

As mentioned earlier, bullying has an effect on physical health. Headaches, stomach issues and sleep deprivation are experienced frequently. These physical symptoms are often expressions of chronic stress. Some young people adopt coping behaviours that increase long-term health risks, such as smoking, using drugs or other harmful habits, as they attempt to manage emotional pain.

Bullying can really disrupt a child's learning and involvement, causing a disruption in their academic career. Kids who face bullying might find themselves avoiding school more often, pulling back from participating in class, and having a harder time with their schoolwork. Over time, this can lead to missing school often or even dropping out, which can close off opportunities and make them feel more hopeless, as if they have failed and it is their fault.

The development of healthy social relationships can also be harmed by bullying. It is possible for victims to struggle with trusting others, withdraw from friendships, or experience difficulties forming and maintaining relationships later in life. This isolation can intensify emotional distress and reduce access to protective social support, which is crucial in a way out of this situation.

Cyberbullying and its unique risks

The rise of social media has introduced new and particularly harmful forms of bullying. Cyberbullying allows harassment to occur at any time, often anonymously, and in front of a potentially large audience. Unlike traditional bullying, which may be limited to only the direct environment, such as a workplace or school, cyberbullying can follow a person anywhere, eliminating whatever was once a place of safety. Online harassment can involve repeated insults, threats, the spread of rumours, or the sharing of embarrassing content. Cyberbullying can intensify feelings of shame and powerlessness, given the public and persistent circumstances. For many adolescents, whose social identity is closely tied to online spaces, this form of bullying can feel inescapable and deeply damaging. Amanda Todd (Canada, 2012) is a clear example of how cyberbullying can lead to suicide. She has been blackmailed online after being coerced into exposing herself on webcam. All the images were repeatedly shared, and because of that, she experienced relentless cyberbullying and harassment. She changed from multiple schools to escape the in-person bullying and harassment, but that did not help either. Even seeking help was not a solution, and the abuse continued online. A few weeks before her death, she posted a YouTube video where she used cue cards to silently describe her experiences, sexual exploitation, depression and self-harm. Lester et al.(2013) found that out of the 10 signs of suicide ideation as described by the American Association of Suicidology, she scored a 9. Amanda died by suicide in October 2012. The case, which is widely known, led to the widespread public awareness of bullying and, in particular, cyberbullying and anti-bullying campaigns in Canada across schools. Criminal prosecution of her online abuser, the Dutch Aydin Coban, followed years later.

Bullying does not automatically lead to suicide, but it can play a powerful role in increasing vulnerability. The constant exposure to bullying can overwhelm a young person's coping abilities. This will be enhanced, particularly if the people being bullied lack dedicated support systems at home, at school, or among peers. The combination of shame, isolation, fear, and helplessness can lead to feelings of entrapment and despair.

The role of adults and support systems

Addressing the relationship between bullying and suicide requires active involvement from parents, caregivers, educators, and other trusted adults. Talking regularly with children and adolescents about their lives, both online and offline, helps identify bullying early and signals that they are not alone. Supportive responses that validate feelings rather than minimise them are crucial. The problem is that bullying often happens secretly or online and is therefore harder to detect. Moreover, the impact it has on the person can be underestimated or overlooked by friends or family.

Schools play a key role in prevention by fostering safe environments, consistently addressing bullying, facilitating classroom discussions, and promoting peer support. Mental health professionals and suicide hotlines can also help or refer people to process their experiences, rebuild self-esteem, and develop healthier coping strategies. Bullying can have grave consequences, but its effects are not inevitable or irreversible.

12 The caregiver

Supporting someone who is thinking about ending their life is a deeply emotional and complex thing to do for anyone who plays the role of a caregiver. There is no one-size-fits-all approach, no guaranteed outcome, and no single action that can ensure the person in crisis's safety. What caregivers can do, however, is offer something powerful and human: presence, shown through patience, humility, and respect for the other person's experience.

Each case is shaped by a unique combination of personal history, emotions, relationships, mental health factors, and immediate circumstances. Because of this, no two situations are exactly alike. The first step for caregivers is to resist the urge to rely on rigid formulas or assumptions. If caregivers have a bias in that situation, it is important to acknowledge it and address it to ensure they listen without prejudice. Listening carefully and responding to the individual in front of you, rather than following a checklist, is essential. Keep in mind that a "successful" outcome is defined by the person who is considering ending their life, not by the caregiver. For some people, success might mean surviving the moment; for others, it might mean feeling heard, understood, having their pain acknowledged, or even ending their lives. Under no circumstances is someone's death a reflection of the caregiver's success or failure. Suicide is a deeply personal act influenced by many forces beyond anyone's control. Caregivers should be cautious about imposing their own ideas of success or failure on the outcome.

Humans are action-oriented. That is why caregivers often feel a strong urge to fix, persuade, argue, or intervene decisively. While this comes from a caring place with all good intentions, it can sometimes backfire. Acting without a clear plan can escalate the situation; rushed solutions might make the person feel that they have not been listened to, misunderstood, pressured, or trapped. Effective caregiving in these moments is about thoughtful responses, too. There is also a risk of burnout if the caregiver tries to handle everything themselves. Working with others on a situation helps to spread the emotional load. Ensure you know and acknowledge your own limits. Asking for help, sharing responsibility, and involving professionals are signs of strength, not weakness.

12.1 The power of time

Time is an interesting concept for caregivers and for people who are attempting to commit suicide. While it is not a cure for the situation, when used thoughtfully, it can be very powerful. By spending time as a caregiver with the person in need, they can build trust. Being present, patient, and genuinely caring helps people in crisis. Building a connection can ease their loneliness, giving them space to process their thoughts and feelings and calm themselves. Many people in crisis are unable to change their thought patterns because their thinking freezes them in time, making them immobile. They will not make changes to their thinking because their thinking is resistant to change. People with suicidal thoughts often deal with complex problems that require time and effort to get out of. Prolonged situations can lead to exhaustion for both caregivers and the person in crisis. Fatigue may blur judgment, diminish emotional control, and cause poor decisions. Extended engagement can also make it more difficult to remain objective. On the other hand, it is good to reward people in need by thanking them for sharing their thoughts and for investing their time in the conversation. Get people to put in as much effort as possible so they will perceive the results as more worthwhile, which might help them step out of the pattern.

Thoughts, emotions, and feelings tend to peak and then slowly fade, and giving someone room to express their pain can help them regain emotional balance. You might see an increase in the use of filler words to buy time for themselves to think, plan, and organise thoughts. Over time, clear thinking can start to reemerge. When someone is overwhelmed, their perspective might be limited; slowing down can help broaden that view. It helps to let the person talk rather than you, and to keep your own time short. The tempo of the conversation has to be set by the person going the slowest. Sometimes, simply allowing time to pass helps de-escalate situations, and the crisis can soften on its own. Patience often proves more effective than pushing for immediate solution results.

The longer a crisis lasts, the greater the risk of exhaustion for both caregivers and the person in crisis. The person attempting to commit suicide might feel more rigid or overwhelmed. Caregivers, on the other hand, might become overly focused on a single solution or be less able to assess risks accurately. Another danger for caregivers is feeling external pressure, such as family input or a deadline. Voss (2016) warns us to resist the urge to respond to a mentioned deadline. Being mindful of acting too fast and taking risks can have big consequences. It is important to pace ourselves, share responsibilities, and stay aware of ourselves.

A caregiver's role is not to control the outcome but to walk alongside someone through their most challenging moments. It is about listening more than talking, patience more than action, and humility more than heroics.

13 I know the end: A conversation with Kirsten Heukels

By Sadiyah Reyal

"I'm going to kill you now."

She said it to her husband. He was dying of cancer. The medical, social and legal systems in the Netherlands that were supposed to help him had spent six months not arriving, not committing, not doing what they had agreed to do. And so, in the end, Kirsten Heukels did what she could. She stood at the bedside of the man she had spent twenty years loving and said, quietly, that she was going to step outside. That she did not think he wanted to die with her in the room. That she was going to the toilet. And then she did what the doctors would not, walked out, told his best friend to go upstairs, and waited, in the way you wait after you have said something irreversible, in the particular silence that only follows the truest thing you have ever done.

I did not know any of this when I sat down to speak with her.

I knew she was a behavioural profiler. A crisis negotiator. A mediator who had spent two decades in the rooms that other people find reasons not to enter. I had read her website, noted her credentials, prepared my questions, and told myself I was the kind of person who could sit across from someone like this without the floor moving under me.

I was wrong.

Kirsten Heukels is not what I expected. She is direct in the way that people are direct when they have long since stopped caring what you think of their directness. She laughs easily and swears without apology. She speaks about death the way most people speak about traffic; not as an inconvenience but as a fact, as something you navigate rather than something you flee.

She did not begin her career in crisis. She began, like so many people who end up in the hardest rooms, by accident. She studied law, quit in the final year because she could see where it was leading and did not want to go there, and found her way into mediation when it was still a novelty in the Netherlands. She took the cases no one else wanted. Divorces, because her colleagues thought the emotions were too much. She loved the emotions. She described them as the best part of us.

From mediation, she moved outward, accumulating tools: culture frameworks, coaching, and body language. Then, in 2012, someone from the National Intelligence Service suggested she look into profiling. Her response was not ambition but genuine bewilderment. 2012 was also the year her husband died, and she had decided to let the idea of profiling wait, to tend to her family first and her work second. But the question stayed with her.

So she looked it up. She first looked at the Mossad, and then her computer overheated, and she remembered there were four children in the house and decided that was not the path. Instead, she taught herself, from scratch, building a method that nobody else had built in quite the same way: hours of footage of humans being humans; without sound first, then the same footage at half speed, because some micro-expressions last only a fraction of a second and the eye cannot catch them at full pace. Then body language. Then, only at the very end, voice. She watches people, she explained, the way you read a letter written in a language you are still learning: slowly, with the sound removed, with all your attention on the shape of the thing rather than the noise of it. Because people nearly never say what they mean at once. And voice, she says, is the most distracting layer of all. The truth moves underneath it, slower, quieter, and if you add the voice too early, it drowns out everything you actually needed to hear.

I found this quite astonishing. The idea that to understand what someone is really feeling, you must first remove the very thing they are using to communicate. That truth moves slower than speech. That if you want to find it, you have to be willing to watch the same moment over and over, at half speed, in silence, until you see what was always there.

She has, I think, been doing this her whole life. Removing the sound first. Slowing everything down. Resisting the pull of the obvious, the spoken, the surface, until the thing underneath becomes visible. It is not just a method for reading people. It is, I would come to understand, her entire philosophy of what it means to be present for someone in pain.

* * *

We were talking about crisis. About the people she has sat with who wanted to die. And she told me something that I have been turning over ever since, something I wrote down, underlined, and have not been able to fully make peace with.

She said: The most important thing is not to try to save someone.

I pushed back. I said:
But that's very difficult to do, isn't it? Especially if this is someone like a family member. Someone you deeply care about. How do you not make it personal?

She did not hesitate.
The most personal thing you can do for somebody you love is to honour their autonomy. So if somebody you love really wants to die, who are you to tell them how?

My instinct, the one I have carried my whole life without ever examining it, is that loving someone in the dark means becoming a wall between them and the harm they are reaching for, that the most loving act is to plant yourself in the doorway and refuse to move, and that this stubbornness is not control but devotion. That, when someone cannot see clearly, your job is to see for them. To make the decision they would make if the pain had not swallowed their thinking whole. I believed this was the way you believe things you have never had to defend, which is to say: completely, and without question.

Kirsten Heukels looked through all of that in about forty seconds.

She told me that what I was describing, the holding on, the deciding for them, the refusal to let go, is not really about the person who is suffering. It is about the person doing the holding. It is about our own terror of loss dressed up as love. And however real that terror is, however human, it fills the room in a way that leaves no air for the person we are trying to reach.

Nobody is interested in what you think or feel, or your judgment. People always make it about them. It is not about you.

I know she is right. That is the maddening part.

Earlier in our conversation, she had laid out her approach towards helping someone in a crisis, what she called 'conditions'. Time. Curiosity. Open questions. I had tried to summarise.

So it's time, curiosity, and questions?

Questions. Open questions.

She sharpened it without hesitation. That small correction said something about how she thinks: precision is not pedantry, it is care. The difference between a question and an open question is the difference between a door held ajar and a door swung wide. I asked whether the purpose of all this was to build empathy. She looked at me the way you look at someone who has almost understood something.

No. Sometimes I don't think empathy is always necessary.

I said: empathy? Out loud, like that, one word, because I did not know what else to say. In a book about suicide prevention, in a chapter about reaching people in crisis, she had just told me that the thing we are all trained to offer, the thing this whole field is built around, was not always necessary. She continued:

Empathy is not even necessary for people to feel heard, seen, or felt. But hearing what they have to say, and really tuning into that, is. It is not about your feeling. It is about your attention.

The carer who floods a crisis conversation with empathy is often, without realising it, filling the space with themselves. What the person in crisis needs is not your emotional resonance. They need the room to be heard. Those are related but not identical, and the difference, in a suicidal crisis, can be the difference between a conversation that opens and one that closes.

I recognise that this sits in some tension with the emphasis on empathy elsewhere in this book. I want to name that rather than smooth it over, because I think Kirsten is pointing at something the clinical literature sometimes misses: that performed empathy - empathy as technique rather than as genuine presence - can become another way of centring yourself. What she is asking for is something quieter and harder. Not feeling for someone. Watching them, in silence, until you see what is actually there.

* * *

She told me about a man. She and her partner were sitting on a terrace in a small Dutch town when he approached them and said, without preamble: I would like to live with you, can I?

He was 66. He had lived with severe Obsessive-Compulsive Disorder since he was eight years old. He had worked at a senior level in a large company, and the condition had cost him decades of what might otherwise have been: the marriage he never had, the children he chose not to want, the promotions he could not reach for, the mornings that other people move through without thinking. For him, OCD was not the mild checking behaviour people imagine when they hear the word. It was a set of rituals that consumed hours of every day, a compulsive logic that his mind could not override, no matter how clearly he understood it was irrational. He lived inside it the way you live inside weather. He had chosen, with a clarity that I found both painful and admirable, not to have children. He did not want to pass on what he carried.

For 38 years, he had been asking for help to die. He had filled every form. He had visited every psychiatrist he could find. Nobody would help him because his suffering was psychiatric rather than physical, and the system that is supposed to offer compassion had drawn its line, and he was on the wrong side of it.

When he told Kirsten he wanted to die, she did not reach for reassurance. She did not tell him his life was worth living or redirect him to a number he could call. She asked him what he had already tried. She asked him how he would like to do it. She told him she thought it was brave that he was saying it out loud.

And then, because he had tried jumping into a harbour twice and stepping onto train tracks once and none of it had worked, she said:

You're at least motivated. That's a really good thing.

I laughed, the involuntary kind that escapes before your judgment catches it. Then I felt guilty for laughing. Then I understood, somewhere below the guilt, that the laugh was actually the correct response, because she had done something in that line that most people spend careers trying to learn and never quite manage: she had met him exactly where he was. Not where she needed him to be. Not where it would be more comfortable for everyone if he were. Exactly where he was, without apology and without flinching, as if his desperation were the most natural thing in the world to sit beside.

They worked together on what she calls scenario thinking: not a technique for talking someone out of dying, but a way of giving back a sense of agency at the moment a person feels they have none left. You lay every possible future side by side without steering toward any of them, and you let the person look. When she asked him to name three scenarios, all three involved dying. Not one involved living. She laughed with him about this because he had the black humour she says she often finds in people who have carried something heavy for a very long time.

I'm going to miss you when you're gone.

She said this to him. Not as a strategy or as a technique to keep him alive. As a fact, offered plainly, because it was true. I have thought about that line more than almost anything else in our conversation. It is the most human thing you can say to someone who has decided the world will be better without them, and it requires nothing except that you mean it.

In the end, the system failed him completely. No doctor would come. He starved himself to death.

She said this plainly, the way she says most things, without softening it or looking away. And then she said:
If I take my cat, who is suffering, to the veterinarian and say life has been sufficient, they will give my cat two injections. One sedative, one final. And in this country, with all the prosperity we claim to have, we don't offer that same respect to human beings.

I thought about him for a long time after our conversation ended. A man who spent a majority of his life asking for a humane death and was given none, who had the rare and terrible self-knowledge to understand exactly what he was and what he carried, who treated strangers on a terrace with more honesty than most people manage in a lifetime. The system that failed him did not fail him out of malice. It failed him out of the same impulse I recognised in myself: the belief that keeping someone alive is always the right thing. That the most loving act is to hold on.

Everyone in his life had heard his voice. The words he used, the requests he made, the forms he filled out, the appointments he kept. They responded to all of it. The doctors applied their criteria. His family gave their love. The system offered its rules. But nobody had done what Kirsten did first, before anything else: removed the sound, slowed it down, and watched in silence long enough to see what was actually underneath. What was underneath was a man who had been carrying the same unbearable weight for nearly four decades and had never, not once, been met where he was.

* * *

I want to tell you something about the person sitting on this side of the conversation. I have learned to talk about suicide with the fluency of someone who has read literature, attended trainings, and discussed reform. The way a person learns to talk about a country they have never actually visited: with confidence, with maps, with the correct vocabulary, and with the private knowledge that none of it is the same as being there. I can sit in a room with professionals and discuss ideation and intervention and means restriction without flinching. I can write chapters about it, which I am doing now, in this book.

But there is another version of this conversation. The one that happens closer in. And in that version, the clinical language dissolves, and what is left is something much harder to hold.

I have had my own dark patches. People I love have had theirs. And in those moments, the distance between knowing the right thing and being able to do it is not a small distance. It is a vast and poorly lit space in which all the frameworks I have learned become very difficult to find.

I tell you this because I think it is important that you know who is writing this chapter. Not an expert observing from the outside.

Someone who is also, in the ways that matter, still navigating the dark. What Kirsten gave me, in the space of one conversation, was not a method. It was a permission. Permission to stop performing certainty. Permission to say: I do not know how to do this perfectly, and I will probably get it wrong, and that is not the same as not trying. Permission to understand that the most useful thing I can offer someone in crisis is not my knowledge or my fear or my desperate love, but my presence. My willingness to sit in the room and not run from what I hear.

She said something near the end of our conversation that I have returned to more than once.
Human energy is one of the strongest things there is. The combination of face, body, and voice, being truly present with someone: nothing will ever replace that.

Not therapy apps. Not crisis lines, though those matter. Not Artificial Intelligence, which she pointed out has already told people to kill themselves. The irreplaceable thing is a human being, fully present, turned toward another human being without an agenda.

That is harder than it sounds. It requires you to let go of the need to fix. To resist the panic that rises when someone says the unsayable. To trust that your presence alone, imperfect and frightened and uncertain as it is, is enough to matter.

* * *

If someone you love has told you they want to die, Heukels offers this: Reach for physical contact first, if it is welcome. Sit with them. Let them feel that you are not going anywhere. Then ask them to tell you all of it. Not the edited version, not the version they think you can handle, but all of it.

Do not perform empathy. Be curious. Ask open questions. Leave space after each answer, because the most important thing is often said into the silence after the first answer, not during it.

And resist, with whatever you have, the impulse to fix it. The scenario thinking she describes, laying out possibilities together without pushing toward any one of them, is something any person can do, not only a trained negotiator. It does not require expertise, but rather presence.

The greatest gift we can give each other is real, sincere human attention. Because it is time, it is effort, it is listening. It is everything.

If you are not sure where to start, she says: start with yourself. Find the one or two people in your life whose opinion you genuinely trust, and go to them. Not to be told what you want to hear, but to be heard. Build your own small network of people who can do for you what you are trying to do for someone else.

And if you are the person in crisis: you are, as she puts it, already here. You already deserve to be here. You do not owe anyone an explanation or an apology for the weight you are carrying. What you need is someone who will sit with you in it. They exist. The world is larger than the room you are in right now.

***

Long before there were helplines or hospitals or crisis protocols, before there were words for what we now call mental health or suicidal ideation, there was this: one person sitting close to another in the dark. Not speaking, necessarily. Not solving. Simply present. It is, as far as we can tell, the oldest technology human beings have for keeping each other alive. Kirsten Heukels did not invent it. She only understood it more clearly than most, named it, and built a practice around it. What she is offering, in everything she has described in this conversation, is not a set of tools for managing a crisis. It is a way of being with another person that most of us knew instinctively as children, and that the noise and speed and fragmentation of modern life has made it very easy to forget.

It takes time. It takes curiosity. It takes the willingness to ask a question and then, which is the harder part, to wait for the real answer. And finally, to accept it.

***

I am going to kill you now.

I have thought about those words more than I expected to. Not with horror, though horror was my first response, that sharp involuntary intake that comes when something violates the script of how love is supposed to look. But underneath the horror was something else, something quieter and harder to name: a kind of awe, the particular kind you feel when you witness a person doing something you are not sure you could do, and then understanding that they did it not because they are built differently from you, not because grief slides off them where it sticks to you, but because they loved someone clearly enough to put that love above their own need to be the one who saved them.

She was selfish and selfless in the same breath, and I have been sitting with the question of whether those two things are actually opposites, or whether, at a certain depth of love, they become indistinguishable. To hold on and let go at once. To love someone loudly enough to go quiet. To be brave enough to walk to the toilet and wait. I do not have a word for that. I am not sure one exists. What I know is that it undoes something in me, the clean certainty I arrived with, the belief that I already understood what love in a crisis was supposed to look like.

What I know is this. Somewhere in a small Dutch town, a man walked up to two strangers on a terrace and told them the truth about his life. And one of those strangers looked at him without flinching, asked him the questions nobody else had thought to ask, sat with him in the full weight of what he was carrying, and did not once try to talk him out of being who he was.

The hardest sentence in this chapter is not the one that opens it. It is the one Kirsten said to the man on the terrace after he told her that all three of his scenarios involved dying.

I'm going to miss you when you're gone.

Not: please stay. Not: your life has value. Not: think of the people who love you. Just: I will miss you. A fact. An offering. With the sound removed, the performance stripped away, nothing left but the truth of one person turning towards another and saying: "You matter to me, whatever you choose."

14 The caregiver or gatekeeper in suicide prevention: roles, responsibilities, and ethics

Caregivers and gatekeepers play a central role in preventing suicide. Those in roles such as healthcare professionals, teachers, first responders, volunteers, clergy, and family members are often the first to notice warning signs and to offer support, help ensure safety, and guide individuals to additional resources. Rudd et al. (2006) state that their job is not to diagnose or treat but to be attentive, compassionate, and ready to act to prevent harm. Since many moments of suicide prevention happen during times when people are at their most vulnerable, the actions of gatekeepers have a profound ethical significance.

Core responsibilities of the gatekeeper

At the core of gatekeeping is being present and attentive. People experiencing suicidal thoughts often feel invisible, unheard, or like a burden. Joiner (2005) highlights that feeling truly understood and connected by gatekeepers can make a substantial difference in reducing suicidal feelings. Gatekeepers play a vital role by listening with care, taking any signs of distress seriously, and responding without judgment. Part of this involves asking direct questions about suicidal thoughts when appropriate. Gould et al. (2005) show that having a conversation about suicide does not increase risk; in fact, it can help by creating space for relief and support.

Ensuring safety is a vital part of our caring role. Gatekeepers play a vital role in reducing immediate risks by encouraging and helping those in need to find protective actions. An example is staying close to the person in crisis, carefully limiting access to dangerous items when possible, and seeking professional support for them. Restricting means is one of the most effective strategies for preventing suicide, especially during intense crises when suicidal thoughts tend to be short-lived (Means Matter, Harvard T.H. Chan School of Public Health; Tishler & Reiss, 2009). Ethically, this aligns with the principle of nonmaleficence; the duty to do no harm.

Understanding ethical principles in suicide prevention

Beauchamp and Childress (2019) state that the right way to prevent suicide rests on four key principles: beneficence, nonmaleficence, autonomy, and justice. Beneficence means that caregivers must act in ways that support and promote the person's well-being, offering kindness, giving them hope, and connections to care. Nonmaleficence reminds us to avoid actions that could cause harm. Examples are: ignoring suicidal remarks, showing shock or disapproval, or leaving the person alone in their crisis.

Respecting autonomy can be challenging because some individuals may express a wish to die as a way of asserting control over unbearable suffering. Hawton and Williams (2001) found that while it is important to respect the person's autonomy, it is equally important to acknowledge that during a severe crisis, judgment can be impaired or blocked by overwhelming pain, depression, a relived trauma, or substance effects. To ensure their safety and protect their life, it is ethically justified to temporarily involve trusted people, mental health professionals or emergency services without the consent of the people themselves. If this approach is going to be followed, it requires sensitivity, openness, and a caring attitude, while making clear that protective measures are driven by concern, not control.

Justice emphasises fair access to support and respectful responses to all people in crisis. The World Health Organisation (2014) points out that gatekeepers need to be aware of the cultural, social, and systemic factors that influence the risk of suicide and help-seeking. This includes stigma, marginalisation, and obstacles to care. Ethical gatekeeping involves advocating for necessary resources and consistently providing support, regardless of age, gender, background, religion, or social status.

Gatekeepers in suicide prevention need to be aware of and understand their own limits. Corey et al. (2015) point out that trying to act as a therapist, promising confidentiality that cannot be kept, or taking full responsibility for someone's safety can unintentionally increase risk. This would not be beneficial for both the person attempting to commit suicide and the gatekeeper. It will help the gatekeeper avoid burnout and moral stress by establishing clear boundaries.

Figley (2002) emphasises that looking after oneself is not optional. A gatekeeper needs to be aware of their ethical responsibilities. Dealing with people who have suicidal thoughts can take an emotional toll on them. It will reduce their effectiveness and trouble their judgment. An ethical practice encourages seeking supervision, debriefing after crises, and caring for our own well-being.

Ethics as acts of human connection

Ultimately, ethics in suicide prevention are about more than rules—they are about showing up for another human being in profound pain. Treating expressions of suicidal feelings with respect, kindness, and understanding affirms the person's worth during moments when they might feel invisible or worthless. As Shneidman (1993) underlined, suicide is often driven by psych ache, not a true wish to die. An ethical gatekeeper recognises this pain and works to reduce feelings of isolation. A gatekeeper will also help keep the person alive longer and show the person in crisis hope and new possibilities.

In this way, the caregiver or gatekeeper becomes a source of moral and emotional support, standing between despair and death, guided by compassion, responsibility, and respect for life.

15 Suicide management

Suicide management is not about being in control or quick fixes. As mentioned in the previous chapter, it is about connection, safety, and shared support. Whether undertaken by caregivers, family members, or professionals, effective suicide management focuses on reducing immediate risk while strengthening hope, resources, and human connection.

What helps in suicide management

Several key elements support people struggling with suicidal thoughts:

- Talking about it: Starting a conversation is where it all starts. An open and honest conversation helps the person in need to get out of isolation and potential shame. Speaking about suicide does not bring someone to an idea: instead, it often provides relief and clarity.
- Sharing with others: It sounds cliché, but sharing is caring. Suicide management is never an effort done by one person only. To spread the responsibility and increase safety, it is almost mandatory to involve trusted people and professionals.
- Watching for safety: A suicide risk assessment should be a standard procedure. Watching for emotional, situational and environmental

clues is essential. The assessment should be repeated, ideally multiple times, to measure progress in either a positive or negative direction.

- Exploring available options: Once the assessment has been made, options can be explored to see what kind of help is needed and help the person with suicidal thoughts see that options do exist. Expanding their windows of tolerance and giving a possible way to get even when they feel trapped.
- A warm handover to professionals: Referrals work best when they are relational rather than abrupt. Staying present with the person in crisis while connecting them with professional help increases trust and follow-through.

The caregiver's role

There are several responsibilities which need to be brought to attention: Firstly, observing: What is visible in the changes in mood, behaviour, or communication that may signal increased risk. Secondly, bringing suicidal thoughts into the discussion: Asking directly and calmly about suicide can open a door that the person may be afraid to open themselves. A question could be: *"Did you ever consider committing suicide?"* Thirdly, seeking help together: The message to the person in need should be: *"You will not be alone, and I will stand beside you as a caregiver/gatekeeper to seek support."* Lastly, following the steps in the intervention: While every situation is unique, suicide management often follows a flexible sequence. A strict order does not fit and will not meet the need at that moment.

Steps

Caregivers should listen to their story without judgment: Let them share their experience in their own words. Feeling heard can reduce emotional intensity. Another step would be to find resources by identifying the appropriate support: mental health professionals, crisis services, family, and friends. Safety first! Focus on immediate safety for the person in crisis. Long-term solutions can wait, as they might not even be prepared for that step. That will be addressed in the follow-up, where caregivers keep in contact with them. It is good to emphasise that gatekeepers and caregivers cannot control the outcome, as it is in the hands of the person considering committing suicide. Accepting that will protect caregivers against guilt and burnout.

Suicide management is about letting the person in crisis make contact with hope: Hope may be small at first. Caregivers can hold hope until the person can feel it themselves, and they have handed the person over to the mental health professionals.

The R.E.L.E.A.S.E - model

The concept was first used by Kevin Briggs, known as the "Guardian of the Golden Gate Bridge." His approach is grounded in lived experience, compassion, and the power of human connection. According to Briggs (2015), the acronym model provides a practical, humane framework for engaging individuals in crisis, emphasising presence over persuasion and connection over control, and helping people in crisis find a way out. R-recognise the indications that a person might need help, such as helplessness, financial struggles or depression. E-engage is about taking part in a conversation with the person. Gather as much information as you can and normalise the feelings. It shows that they are not alone. L-listen in the model requires patience, silence, and full attention, allowing the individual to express their story at their own pace. Only then can you understand. Listening, in this sense, becomes a life-preserving act. E-empathise involves deeply understanding and acknowledging the individual's emotional pain without judgment, correction, or minimisation. People in crisis do not want to be fixed; they want to be acknowledged. A-accept them as they are without being judgmental or condescending. Still drive the conversation in a positive direction. S-support emphasises connecting individuals to ongoing help, resources, and relationships, ensuring they are not left alone after the immediate crisis. E-encourage them to find the help they need after the immediate intervention is over. Standing next to them in seeking help is essential until the mental health professionals or social workers take over.

A note on helping

People who are considering suicide often genuinely need help and may feel thankful. For some of them, it is still hard to accept help. When helping in a crisis, it shows we have enough resources to share, but it can also suggest that the person receiving help depends on our kindness. Nadler (2002) suggests that this can create a sense of inequality, with the helper perceived as having higher status and the person receiving help feeling vulnerable or less powerful. Such differences can make giving help feel like an expression of status and control, and receiving help can even be a little intimidating or uncomfortable for the recipient.

16 Culture

Wherever we go, we are lucky to meet people from all sorts of backgrounds. These backgrounds shape who they are, influenced by deep-seated beliefs and implicit theories that guide how they see the world and act fascinatingly, these are learned yet keep evolving and are often rationalised. As caregivers, we have the key role of navigating through this rich diversity. We might only be aware of what is visible, like clothing or diet, but inside each person, there is an entire world-ways of solving problems, how they organise their time, and what they value in friendships. All of this falls under the beautiful umbrella of culture. The National Center for Cultural Competence (2001) describes culture as:

"An integrated pattern of human behaviour which includes but is not limited to—thought, communication, languages, beliefs, values, practices, customs, courtesies, rituals, manners of interacting, roles, relationships, and expected behaviours of an ethnic group or social groups whose members are uniquely identifiable by that pattern of human behaviour."

Cultural intelligence

In today's world, it is crucial to have cultural intelligence as part of your caregiver skill set, alongside emotional intelligence. However, what is cultural intelligence?

Oxford Review (2025) describes it as: "the ability to effectively understand, adapt, and work in different cultural contexts. It goes beyond basic cultural awareness by focusing on how individuals navigate and succeed in culturally diverse environments. Cultural intelligence includes skills in perceiving cultural differences, adjusting behaviour, and making decisions that consider cultural nuances, which are essential for successful collaboration in globalised settings."

There are four aspects in cultural intelligence: knowledge, mindfulness, skills and motivation.

Cultural knowledge

People's perspectives on suicide can vary a lot from one culture to another. These views can shape our personal motivation and influence the unspoken social rules, expectations, and standards of acceptable behaviour, which are known as social norms. In countries where Islam is deeply rooted in the culture, for example, you will find that suicide rates are generally low because the Qur'an considers it an unforgivable act, except in the context of war, where it relates to martyrdom. In Western cultures, on the other hand, suicide has often been viewed negatively. It was even illegal, and those who survived attempts could face imprisonment. This is different from some Asian cultures like Japan, where suicide can be seen as a part of a tradition, such as hara kiri or seppuku. In these cases, it might be considered an act of honour, such as a kamikaze attack. Meanwhile, in India, suicide is a sensitive and shameful issue, surrounded by stigma. It is condemned when seen as a selfish act, as many scriptures, such as the Bhagavad Gita and the Upanishads, suggest, but it is also sometimes glorified, as in the historical practice of Sati, where widows would self-immolate.

Cultural mindfulness

Kabigting (2022) gives us the following definition: "a state of being mindful of, first, your own cultural construct, and second, the cultural constructs of the other person you are interacting with at any given moment." It is vital that potential preconceptions or biases not influence the conversation as a caregiver. It will be a challenge, especially when the conversation conflicts with our own beliefs, norms, and values."

Cultural skills or competencies

This is defined as a set of values, behaviours, attitudes, and practices within a system, organisation, program, or among individuals that enables them to work effectively cross-culturally. Further, it refers to the ability to honour and respect the beliefs, language, interpersonal styles and behaviours of individuals (Denboba, 1993). Empathy, effective engagement, and active listening are crucial competencies for having a proper conversation in any culture, especially in cross-cultural conversations.

Cultural motivation

The best way to think of it is that it involves a person's actions, desires, and needs to learn about and connect with culture-based incentives that are really important in their life, like work or family. These can be different for each person compared to the group as a whole. Things like identity and feeling a sense of belonging or cultural fit influence motivation. It is also helpful to be aware of potential obstacles, such as stigmas or misunderstandings.

As a caregiver, building a meaningful connection with the person is so important. First, from the heart, with openness, acceptance, and encouragement. Then, from the mind, by understanding perceptions, interpretations, and insights. And finally, from the body, through gestures, expressions, and actions (Early et al, 2004).

It is helpful to remember that during stressful situations, people tend to turn to their cultural roots for comfort. Having a global mindset is truly valuable because it helps you recognise, interpret, and adapt to various cultural signals- whether obvious or subtle, familiar or unfamiliar. This ability ensures that your effectiveness is not hindered when working with people from diverse backgrounds around the world. Plus, it opens up a world of opportunities you might not have expected, allowing you to explore new possibilities with confidence. (Solomon, C. M., and Schell, M. S., 2009).

16.1 A story: Both sides now

Culture shapes not only who we are but also how we understand and experience mental health. It influences how we fall into illness and how we emerge from it. Some cultures view mental health struggles as a consequence of past karma, while others recognise them as genuine medical conditions that require care and treatment. In certain societies, the path to healing is through devotion and divine intervention, while others rely on therapy and medication. Some cultures refuse to acknowledge mental health issues altogether, attributing them instead to spiritual disconnection.

During one of his therapy sessions, Luke was presented with a thought-provoking perspective. He came from a culture where marrying a relative, no matter how distant, was strictly forbidden. To him, seeking a life partner outside of his family and extended kin felt natural, unquestionable even. Then, he met Samir, a close friend from a culture where marrying a first cousin was not only accepted but often encouraged.

At first, Luke was bewildered, unable to comprehend how something that felt so unnatural to him could be entirely normal for someone else. His therapist used this as an example of cultural differences. How what seems ordinary to one person may be deeply unsettling to another. For Samir, marrying within the family was a norm; for Luke, the very thought was unimaginable.

This is the beauty of cultural diversity. Our perceptions of normal are not universal but shaped by the worlds we grow up in. And just as culture influences traditions, it also shapes how we understand and approach mental well-being.

17 The central role of trust in suicide prevention

Trust plays a vital role in suicide prevention to be successful. For those experiencing suicidal thoughts, connecting with a suicide prevention gatekeeper often happens during very vulnerable moments filled with fear and uncertainty about life. Michel et al. (2017) show that trust, or the absence of trust, to a large extent affects whether people feel comfortable sharing their thoughts and emotions, seeking support, and accepting help that could potentially save their lives. Building trust is not just about one thing; it develops through kind and respectful actions that make someone feel safe and cared for.

To help reduce the fear and confusion of people considering suicide, it is important as a gatekeeper to communicate clearly, openly, and honestly. When gatekeepers take the time to explain their role, what confidentiality and neutrality mean, and what might happen next, people in despair are less likely to feel pressured or betrayed. Being honest, even when the news is not easy, helps to strengthen trust by showing respect for the person's right to know and understand. Rogers et al. (2018) found that open, transparent communication encourages cooperation and makes suicide risk assessments and interventions more effective. Frei and Morriss (2020) add that what you say should be logical, which means that the skills, arguments, and ideas have to make sense to the people in need.

As Walker (2008) points out, creating trust involves several key elements: reciprocity, mutual respect, shared decision-making, altruism, and valuing the person's own experience. Trust grows stronger when gatekeepers are transparent and reliable. It is crucial for them, too, to always keep their promises. Another way to increase trust is to show integrity. Actions have to be based on values, and all decisions are guided by ethics. Being dependable, showing up consistently, and responding when promised are especially crucial for those with histories of abandonment or betrayal. Baldwin et al. (2007) argue that reliable care helps to build a stronger relationship and can even help to reduce the risk of suicide. Trust is about authenticity: being perceived as an honest and genuine person. As a gatekeeper, it is important to respect people's self-determination, which does not mean that people in crisis do not need help, given the fact that the relationship between a gatekeeper and a person considering suicide is not equal in responsibility. Jobes (2016) found that genuinely caring for the individual's well-being helps counteract fears of judgment, punishment, or dismissal. When people feel genuinely cared for rather than treated as just part of a procedure, they are more likely to open up about suicidal thoughts and work together on safety plans.

At the heart of trust is empathy, the capacity to truly understand and communicate understanding of someone else's emotions. Empathy affirms their pain without endorsing self-harm and shows that they are not alone. Both Rogers (1957) and Norcross and Wampold (2011) found that strong empathic engagement has been linked to less suicidal thinking, greater help-seeking, and stronger therapeutic relationships. For many individuals, feeling genuinely heard and understood can be a vital factor in choosing life.

There is one area where a gatekeeper has no influence in building trust: the brain. Kosfeld et al. (2005) show that the hormone oxytocin, a key biological driver, is associated with trust. The stress a person in crisis experiences inhibits trust, thereby reducing trust levels and the quality of social interactions.

To conclude, be aware as a gatekeeper that whenever people meet for the first time, their brains automatically categorise them, male or female, same or different, friend or foe, to predict if they can trust that person and what is likely to happen next. In those first seconds, people unconsciously decide whether or not to trust. Once people are convinced that someone is or is not to be trusted, they will reinforce our judgment.

18 Empathy

Empathy is one of the most essential skills a caregiver needs. Hodges and Myers (2007) describe it as:
"Understanding another person's experience by imagining oneself in that other person's situation: One understands the other person's experience as if it were being experienced by the person himself, but without himself experiencing it."

There are two important aspects to empathy: cognitive and affective empathy. Brown (2021) explains that cognitive empathy helps people to recognise and understand another person's feelings, while affective empathy involves truly connecting with their experience. Knowing the difference is especially helpful for suicide gatekeepers and caregivers, as it guides them to respond with care without becoming overwhelmed in high-risk situations. Cognitive empathy helps gatekeepers identify, interpret, and make sense of emotions like hopelessness, fear, or a sense of being trapped, without taking those feelings on themselves. It enables accurate risk assessments, supports conversation management, and supports thoughtful decision-making. On the other hand, affective empathy lets gatekeepers genuinely connect with someone's feelings, showing warmth, validation, and sincere care. This helps the person in crisis feel truly seen, heard, and understood. Feelings of isolation and suicidal thoughts are likely to be reduced when this behaviour is shown. When someone in crisis feels emotionally understood, they are more open to sharing their thoughts and accepting support.

Caregivers and gatekeepers must find a balance between the two. Only using cognitive empathy without emotional connection can be perceived by the carereceiver as cold or dismissive. On the other hand, relying too much on affective empathy can lead to personal stress or burnout. A mix of both worlds will lead to a balanced understanding of empathy.

Empathetic strategies

Empathetic strategies are the welcoming ways people communicate to show understanding and care. Using one or more of the strategies mentioned below can help them build emotional bonds, offer validation, and strengthen their connections with others.

A common empathetic strategy is acknowledging parallel experience, which involves revealing that one has experienced something similar to what a person in crisis has. Sharing a related experience creates a bond between the person in crisis and the gatekeeper. Saying, for example: *"The same thing happened to me last year,"* conveys solidarity and reduces perceived emotional distance. Burleson (2010) explains that this strategy can normalise emotions and build rapport, if not overused. If used too often, this strategy or inappropriate self-focus can undermine empathy. If such disclosures are made, they must be brief and clearly supportive of the person in crisis. Remember, it is not about the caregiver but about the person in need. Self-disclosure truly helps foster a sense of connection. Jourard (1971) emphasises that it can help to break down the (perceived) power differences and build trust. Opening up in a genuine way by the gatekeeper, showing vulnerability and authenticity, can encourage the other person to be more open as well.

Another strategy is response cries. Response cries are short verbal expressions or sounds, such as *"Ah!"* or *"Sigh"*. Such words help to build rapport with the person in need. Goffman (1981) underlines the importance of these utterances as they demonstrate attentiveness and a shared emotional stance. Another advantage is that these minimalist encouragers do not interrupt the speaker. This reduces the chance of a change in the narrative.

Understanding claims is also an empathetic strategy. It is a clear way to show a person relates to someone's feelings or experiences. An example is saying, *"I can completely comprehend that."* These understanding claims can make conversations feel more comforting and can serve as a validation, especially when emotions are running high. Clark (1996) warns that saying, "I understand" without actually listening to what has been said, might come across as presumptuous or overlook the other person's feelings. To be most helpful, paraphrasing or labelling emotions can support these claims, so the other person feels truly heard and understood.

Subjunctive assessments work as an empathetic strategy, too. Batson (2009) suggests that it helps because of perspective-taking and imagining the other person's viewpoint. An example of this is: "I would feel the same way if they had told that to me." It also acknowledges emotional reactions without claiming that experiences are identical, making it especially helpful in delicate or uncertain situations, such as a suicide attempt.

Labelling someone's emotions is a favourite strategy of Chris Voss (2016). It means describing what their emotional state seems like or how it sounds, such as saying, *"It sounds as though you are feeling really frustrated."* Goleman (1995) explains that this step helps the person feel acknowledged and understood, while also encouraging emotional clarity and better regulation. When people accurately label their emotions, it can lead to more thoughtful reflection and a sense of being understood. This is especially important during conversations about suicide and can invite the person in crisis to tell more, which also improves their problem-solving skills. The shared understanding will also reduce the conflict within themself of the suicidal person.

Tactical empathy

Tactical empathy, according to Chris Voss (2016), is about: "intentionally recognising, acknowledging, and naming someone else's emotions."

Empathy is understanding the other person's emotions, not necessarily liking or agreeing with them, and articulating that understanding. Nowadays, empathy is often confused with sympathy and compassion. Empathy is about the transmission of information; compassion is a reaction to that transmission. Tactical empathy should be looked at as a can-do, either do good or bad, depending on how you use it. Dark empaths, for example, are people who score high on cognitive empathy but lack affective empathy, using their insight to manipulate, control, or exploit others for personal gain.

In practice, tactical empathy is shown through kind language that appreciates someone's feelings without judging or arguing. Phrases like "I understand that you do not want to live anymore" or *"This must be hard"* show that we recognise how deeply someone is hurting and that their feelings matter. Calling out emotions directly, say, *"You are in a lot of pain. Let us talk"*, can help lessen emotional overload by making what is unspoken clearer. This kind of emotional labelling often soothes the nervous system and invites more openness.

Tactical empathy also taps into curiosity and carefully chosen questions to create an open, safe space. Using phrases like *"It seems to me that a lot is going on. What can you tell me?"* or *"You feel trapped, what does that mean?"* encourages the other person in crisis to share more of their story without feeling interrogated or judged. To show you understand the other person, you can use validations such as *"That is right. Life does suck. Tell me more about how terrible things feel"*. Chris Voss (2016) underlines that, "That is right is what we say when we feel completely heard, and there is a chemical change that takes place in our brain, but when you would say, 'You are right, what they are really saying to you is, 'Please, shut up. Stop talking. I cannot take it anymore. Go away.'"

Using techniques that are a part of tactical empathy, such as labelling, mirroring, validating, and asking open-ended questions, helps create a safe and welcoming space while building a stronger connection. When people feel understood, they tend to open up more, become less defensive, and are more willing to engage. In serious situations such as crisis intervention or suicide prevention, tactical empathy can be an immensely helpful tool for calming things down, building trust, and making individuals feel less alone in their struggles.

19 Listening

Listening is one of the most difficult things to do, which is built around communication, relationships, decision-making, and psychological well-being. Rogers and Farson (1957) and Brownell (2012) show that effective listening enhances trust, reduces conflict, and improves outcomes in personal and professional contexts. People tend to forget that listening is an active process rather than a passive one, as it requires intention, presence, and skill.

The five levels of listening

Rosenbaum (2017) views listening as a process unfolding across five progressive levels, each reflecting increasing depth and engagement.

1. **Ignoring:** The listener is physically present but mentally disengaged. Attention has not been given to the speaker. The message it displays is "you are not important to me."
2. **Responsive:** The listener appears attentive through nonverbal cues but is internally distracted. Just waiting for your turn to talk.
3. **Judging:** The listener hears only parts of the message that confirm existing beliefs or interests before they even hear the entire story. The message is "Here is the problem."

4. **Reflective:** The listener focuses on the speaker's words and meaning, seeking understanding. The message is "What can I take away?"
5. **Empathising/Resonant:** The listener is fully present and open, allowing both the speaker and the listener to be changed by the interaction. The message here is "what are you experiencing?"

Linear listening and associative listening

Listening can also be understood in terms of cognitive processing styles. These styles are linear and associative listening. Linear listening is all about structure, a focus on facts, logic, and outcomes. This style can be helpful in problem-solving, instruction, and decision analysis. Associative listening is meaning-oriented. Brownell (2012) explains that listeners with this style are all about connection. That can be with ideas, emotions, and memories. It is also helpful to note the underlying themes or needs as the speaker speaks. While linear listening prioritises clarity and efficiency, associative listening focuses on empathy, creativity, and deeper emotional understanding. Caregivers and gatekeepers should develop both skills, as this will help them shift flexibly between these modes as the conversation with the person in crisis unfolds.

Transformative listening

Transformative listening, according to Rosenbaum (2017), is a warm, intentional way of listening in which the listener thoughtfully pauses, gives their full attention, and creates an environment that puts the speaker's ideas at the centre. It all starts with trust, the real belief that the other person already has the wisdom and insight to discover their own solutions. This kind of listening is based on genuine interest, with the listener staying fully present, curious, and engaged rather than distracted or trying to solve the issues in advance. Most importantly, transformative listening offers space, time, silence, and psychological safety for the speaker to reflect and elevate their thinking about the situation. It takes a lot of patience to transform the conversation from negativity to hope,a skill a caregiver must have.

Watson et al. (1995) identify four primary listening styles. Each style has strengths and limitations, and effective communicators adapt their listening style to the demands of the situation.

- **Analytical listening:** The focus is on facts, accuracy, detail, and logical consistency. The evaluation of the facts is done without any bias or prejudice.
- **Relational listening:** The focus is on the relation within the conversation. Connection and emotional understanding are key, with the help of (tactical) empathy.
- **Critical listening:** The focus is on evaluating the speaker's verbal content for credibility, bias, and persuasive intent.
- **Task-focused listening:** The focus is goal-oriented and efficient, concentrating on information necessary to complete specific tasks.

Active listening

Rogers and Farson (1957) define active listening as a thoughtful practice that combines paying close attention, thoughtful reflection, and responsive feedback. To ensure true understanding, paraphrasing, reflecting emotions, summarising, and asking questions are used without being judgmental. Weger et al. (2014) show that active listening can improve relationship satisfaction, help reduce misunderstandings, and create a sense of psychological safety in conversations. It conveys the message that what others have to say is valuable. Active listening is first about understanding the other person, then about being understood as the listener.

There are signs that can hinder a person's ability to listen actively. That could happen if the person who should be listening is talking more than the speaker, or if they are giving advice and suggesting solutions without first listening to the entire story. What a caregiver or gatekeeper should never do is tell people in crisis not to feel the way they do or to zone out when the person in need is displaying a negative attitude.

The power of silence

Silence is often underestimated. It is instead a powerful skill to use in conversation with people. When intentionally chosen by caregivers, silence can create a nurturing space that provides the people in need time to reflect. Through that reflection, hidden feelings, emotions, or needs can emerge. Silence invites people in need to be more aware of that without pressure. Hill et al. (2003) found that silence is often more effective than verbal responses in fostering insight, conveying empathy, and showing respect. At the same time, caregivers need to be aware of the different interpretations of silence among cultures. Silence in Japan, for example, can last for six seconds in a conversation, while in the USA it lasts, on average, a mere two seconds.

20 What questions to ask?

Asking questions is a crucial skill for caregivers or gatekeepers supporting someone who is suicidal or contemplating suicide. Thoughtful questions can get the person in crisis, who is often suffering in silence, into a shared understanding. Contrary to fears, both Gould et al. (2005) and Dazzi et al. (2014) indicate that directly asking about suicide does not elevate suicidal thoughts. They found that it lessens distress by showing care, respect, and a readiness to confront tough truths together.

When a person in distress shares something vague or raises a concern, asking gentle clarifying questions can make a big difference. For example, if they say, *"Soon I will not be here anymore,"* it might mean different things. 'Soon' can indicate that an imminent action will be taken by thinking about hurting themselves, or they are feeling emotionally overwhelmed. By asking, *"What do you mean by soon?"* a caregiver or gatekeeper shows they care and want to understand what the person is going through. Joiner et al. (2009) highlight that asking such a question is important for assessing risks and determining the best way to support them.

Getting connected and staying connected with loved ones is important for supporting the person considering suicide. To highlight such relationships, one might consider asking questions such as: *"How would the people you leave behind feel?"* or *"Whom would you miss most?"* Joiner (2005) and Kleiman and Liu (2013) warn that these questions should never be used to induce guilt and recommend asking them. It is not to emphasise the social disconnection but to remind them of their meaningful connections and that their presence is important to others, which is a vital protective factor against suicide.

It is important to understand the story behind the person in crisis, as Michel et al. (2017) explain. Creating a safe space and giving them the time they need helps to ease the emotional and cognitive overload. Some questions the caregiver can ask include *"What has led up to all this?"* or *"How was it in the past compared to now?"* This allows the caregiver and the person in crisis to recognise patterns, turning points and past coping methods.

Jobes (2016) points out that exploring feelings of ambivalence helps in suicide prevention, as it can reduce suicidal thoughts. Asking questions like *"What is holding you back from ending your life?"* or *"What has helped you keep going for so long?"* shows empathy. More importantly, it also recognises their desire to live or their hope for change.

Stanley and Brown (2012) suggest that such present-focused conversations can greatly reduce suicidal behaviour, especially when approached in a collaborative manner rather than being direct or commanding. Questions which can help are: *"How are we going to make sure that you will be safe tonight?"* or "What do you need to ensure that you will still be around tonight?"

Hypothetical questions are questions that let the person with suicidal thoughts dream and help keep hope alive. These questions begin with *"What if"* or *"Imagine"*. Examples are: *"If you were to get out of this situation, what would that mean to you?"* or *"Imagine you were free from the emotional pain, what impact would that have on you?"* The follow-up question could then be: *"What do you need to get to that point?"*

21 Connecting with neurodiverse people in crisis

Neurodiverse people face notably higher rates of suicidal thoughts and behaviours compared to the general population. Both Cassidy et al. (2018) and Hirvikovski et al. (2020) found that the increased risk is not due to neurodivergence itself but is closely tied to ongoing misunderstandings, social exclusion, emotional challenges, and repeated feelings of invalidation. Traditional conversation styles that rely on common assumptions about emotional sharing, speech fluency, or reciprocity might unintentionally make things harder for neurodiverse individuals when they are in deep distress. For caregivers and suicide prevention gatekeepers, connecting effectively during an intervention does not stop with only words; it is more important how we communicate as a whole. This chapter focuses on how conversation management works with those with Attention Deficit Hyperactivity Disorder (ADHD) and autism. That does not mean there is no acknowledgement of other neurodivergent people, but rather a choice of the writers, since most misunderstandings are around them.

So how can gatekeepers adjust their conversation approaches to support better neurodiverse people who are struggling with suicidal thoughts, with particular focus on the differences between those with ADHD and autistic people?

To begin, many may express their feelings indirectly. Behaviours such as silence, irritability, or keeping conversations factual are common, especially among people with autism. Brown (2013) found that others, such as those with ADHD, are more likely to show their distress more suddenly and at a higher intensity. At the same time, caregivers and gatekeepers should be aware that relying solely on a single typical emotional signal can lead them to miss or misinterpret it.

When talking with people with ADHD who are experiencing suicidal distress, they might show very strong emotions, racing thoughts, or trouble focusing. In such situations, it is important to slow the pace of speech, as it is hard for them to digest the verbal content. Using straightforward language and keeping things simple will also improve the quality of the conversation while keeping them engaged. Circling back to the racing thoughts, people with ADHD may suddenly go through suicidal impulses, which can cause the situation to escalate quickly. According to Theodore P. Beauchaine et al. (2020), financial distress is associated with a fourfold higher risk of suicide among those with ADHD.

People with autism who are considering suicide often go through intense distress caused by feelings of social exhaustion and loneliness. This can also trigger a so-called sensory overload, meaning the brain is overwhelmed by senses: taste, smell, touch, sight, or sound. The emotional pain is not clearly expressed, making them feel even more misunderstood. Autistic people might show it through logical thoughts, saying they are done or zone out, leading to complete withdrawal, which is normally expressed through emotional words. Therefore, using a clear, predictable, and literal style of communication is very helpful.

Caregivers and gatekeepers who support autistic people in crisis should avoid using metaphors, idioms, or implied meanings. The use of that can sometimes cause more confusion and distress, as figurative language is not clear to them. Asking direct questions about safety and suicidal thoughts is more beneficial and comforting since it helps clear up any uncertainty. Kerns et al. (2015) note that it is crucial to use multiple communication methods. Examples are respecting their need for less eye contact or texting instead of a conversation. NICE (2022) also suggests reducing physical proximity or speaking in a softer tone to reduce sensory overload.

Key Differences in Approach: ADHD vs Autism

	ADHD	AUTISM
Communication pace	Often rapid, pressured	Often slower, deliberate
Primary risk pathway	Impulsivity, emotional dysregulation	Social isolation, chronic invalidation
Helpful strategies	Structure, grounding, focus support	Clarity, predictability, and literal language
Emotional expression	Intense, fluctuating	Internalised, logical, or muted
Gatekeeper focus	Slowing down, reducing overload	Reducing ambiguity, sensory safety

While these distinctions are helpful, gatekeepers must avoid stereotyping. Individual preferences should guide all interactions. While in earlier chapters of this book, suicide risk assessments were introduced, it is good to keep in mind that these assessments might overlook the needs of neurodiverse people, especially when they focus heavily on verbal skills, emotional labelling, and quick responses.

21.1 A story: Born this way

"There are seven billion versions of normal on this planet."
Matt Haig

Obviously, with the world population now exceeding 8 billion, that number has only grown. The very sense of humanity lies in its diversity. No two minds are the same. If we were all identical, we would be like machines, wired and programmed to function identically. But that is not the truth. The truth is that we are not made of the same metal; the same mould does not mould us. Each one of us is unique. We are shaped by experiences, perceptions, and the culture that we belong to.

There is a Netflix show called "Never Have I Ever", starring Devi Vishwakumar. In the show, she struggles with trauma and PTSD after her father's death and begins therapy. Obviously, therapy covers more than just her father's death, and her trauma expands into everyday life. It teaches her how to navigate daily challenges, ground herself, and feel okay with who she is and who she is becoming.

At one point, Devi asks her therapist about why she feels so much sadness, why she feels very different from others, and why she feels so problematic. And her therapist replies: "Devi, you feel a lot, which means sometimes you are going to hurt a lot. But it also means that you are going to live a life that is emotionally rich and really beautiful."

Now, this is definitely not an attempt to romanticise feeling sad or to normalise it in any unhealthy way. It is also very different from being neurodivergent. Feeling emotions very deeply or being empathetic is not the same as being clinically neurodivergent, but the line can sometimes feel thin, and diagnosis is more complicated.

The point is that being neurodivergent, or being around someone who is, is okay. It is very human. One is not inferior to the other, and the other is not superior. Both experiences are valid. What matters is recognising neurodiversity. It deserves to be acknowledged, understood, and respected.

22 Stress

If there is one thing that will happen in a suicide situation, it is stress. Not only with the person considering suicide but with caregivers and gatekeepers as well. Nevertheless, what is actually stress? Stress is a physiological and psychological response that occurs when people perceive demands as exceeding their coping abilities. It is your body's reaction to a challenge or a demand. Arnsten (2009) and Lupien et al. (2009) show that stress disrupts cognitive processes in the prefrontal cortex, where cognitive and impulse control, decision-making, and emotional regulation occur, and in the hippocampus, where memory and stress regulation occur. These disruptions can lead to measurable declines in intellectual performance. The stress response system activates hormonal and neural systems designed to promote survival. At the same time, sustained activation of these systems can impair brain regions responsible for intellectual functioning. A few effects should be highlighted to better understand yourself as a caregiver in stressful situations and as the person in despair.

McEwen (2017) found that slowed thinking is one such effect. The reason is that attention will be allocated to perceived threats rather than to cognitive processing. Elevated cortisol levels, the body's main stress hormone, interfere with neural signalling in the prefrontal cortex. This will result in delayed responses and difficulty in processing complex information. Another effect is a poor attention span and difficulty focusing. McEwen and Morrison (2013) explain that stress-related imbalances in neurotransmitters cause this, the body's chemical messengers. For caregivers and gatekeepers, this means that their attentiveness during the conversations may decline significantly. Confusion and disorientation may also happen as a result of high stress levels. Be aware that in suicide situations, it is harder for the person in distress to organise their thoughts and to follow instructions given by the gatekeepers or caregiver. This will be even more difficult in circumstances requiring rapid thinking or multitasking. Lupien et al. (2009) note that chronic stress further intensifies these effects.

A similar conclusion was found by McEwen (2017), who found that it also applies to memory, particularly working memory and recall. As mentioned earlier, the hippocampus is highly sensitive to stress hormones. For a person contemplating suicide, it might be difficult to go back to the time when these thoughts were not present. This is due to the impaired retrieval of the knowledge stored in the brain. Learning new information, such as how to move away from suicidal thoughts, might be difficult as well, while stress levels are still high. Last but not least, it is good to mention that stress may also result in having nightmares or obsessive thinking. These mental experiences consume so many cognitive resources that they can weaken critical thinking and bias thinking. Arnsten (2009) argues that stress can also lead to difficulties with word-finding, as language-related brain networks are disrupted.

All these intellectual effects of stress are linked and reinforce each other. It will take time to stop that domino effect, especially in suicide conversations. Having the actual conversation and helping them understand that you, as a caregiver and gatekeeper, are there to help them find a solution to get out of the situation can reduce their stress levels and stimulate their cognitive abilities.

23 Coping with stress

Caregivers and gatekeepers who support people considering suicide or actively trying to end their lives are, sometimes over an extensive period, under very intense emotional and psychological pressure. They need to stay calm, attentive, and compassionate during moments when every step in the conversation feels crucial. Everly and Mitchell (2008) highlight that handling stress well in these situations is not just about personal well-being. Stress also affects judgment, presence, and the safety of those being helped. So, what can help manage that stress?

One of the simplest but most effective tools caregivers and gatekeepers use to manage stress is breathing. Seppälä et al. (2020) showed that practising breathing exercises and mindfulness can lead to better mental health and positive emotions, and alleviate stress and depression. Philipot et al. (2010) suggest that our brain associates different emotions with different breathing patterns. If caregivers and gatekeepers practice breathing exercises, they trick their brains into thinking their emotional state is different from what it actually is. When people are happy, their breathing is regular and steady. However, when they are stressed, anxious, or fearful, their breathing becomes irregular, shallow, and quicker. When slowing down breathing during times of stress, the brain can be misled, tricking it into thinking a person is actually in a calm state and that there is no threat or challenge at hand.

McEwen (2007) points out that in high-risk suicide situations, the body's stress response can kick in very quickly, activating the sympathetic nervous system and making it harder to think clearly and stay emotionally balanced. Taking deep, intentional breaths helps calm physiological arousal, activate the parasympathetic nervous system, and restore a sense of inner control. Van der Kolk (2014) notes that controlled breathing is a powerful method for reducing stress and maintaining emotional steadiness under pressure.

Another way to cope with stress is self-control, which plays a key part in the caring approach in preventing suicide. Self-control is all about the ability to manage emotional reactions during conversations in suicide situations. Managing emotional reactions does not mean the person has to suppress their feelings or remain detached from the crisis. Caregivers and gatekeepers often face strong emotions from the person considering suicide. These emotions could be, for example, anger, despair, fear, or blame. If caregivers or gatekeepers take these reactions personally, they can quickly become overwhelmed by those reactions. Shneidman (1996 notes that, by staying in control of their emotions, staying calm, and keeping focus, caregivers and gatekeepers can better support the person in crisis, especially when there is an immediate risk or potential loss of life. Taking a moment to pause and reflect can help cope with stress and to (re)gain self-control. This can be accomplished by having a few seconds of silence in your conversations about suicide while asking yourself the question, *"How am I feeling right now?"* Being aware of your emotional state can help you remain composed and effective in challenging situations. Slowing down the conversation is also a good stress-management technique that works well with effective suicide intervention. When the situation becomes intense, caregivers can intentionally slow their pace, speak more gently, steady their voices, and allow for moments of silence. Everly and Mitchell (2008) found that slowing down prevents people from making impulsive decisions and encourages thoughtful, measured responses that focus on safety, connection, and support, rather than rushing through the moment.

When possible, taking a short break can be a helpful way to reduce stress. Suicide gatekeepers do not need to stay in a constant state of crisis; they can benefit from stepping back, whether by passing on responsibilities or taking a moment for themselves. People know breaks are helpful, but they do not always take them. A lot of people think that because a break makes them feel better, it will make them perform better. Helton et al. (2017) emphasise that this is not necessarily true. If a caregiver or gatekeeper wants to disengage themselves from a conversation in a suicide situation, that is okay. Southwick and Charney highlight that disengagement is not about giving up. Disengagement is about protecting your well-being so you can continue caring effectively and reduce the chance of burnout.

Another way to cope with stress is by shifting your focus. When caregivers and gatekeepers tune out their own reactions and instead listen fully, paying close attention to the person's story, feelings, and meaning, it not only lowers personal stress but also builds trust and connection. For those supporting others, managing stress is intricately linked to the vital task of protecting life. By managing their own stress, they protect themselves and the person they are helping, ensuring that their compassion and presence are strong when they matter most. The checklist below might be helpful at times to keep you aware of the situation and safe. This list can also be applied to the person considering suicide.

- **Orientation:** Does the person know who or where he/she is?
- **Thinking:** Is their thinking clear and realistic? Do you notice their eyes darting or fixed, hinting at their clarity? Sensory cues provide important insight into their state of mind.
- **Emotions:** Are their emotions appropriate to the situation?
- **Body movements:** Are their posture, movements or gestures bizarre?
- **Sensory disorders:** Do they seem to lack the usual sensory awareness?
- **Awareness of other people:** Are they aware of how other people react to them?
- **Self-control:** Do they seem to be in control of their thoughts, speech, and movements?

Moreover, finally, a caregiver or gatekeeper can also keep a diary to manage the stress. Newman (2020) found that journaling works on two levels, both related to our feelings and thoughts. First, it is a way of expressing emotions rather than stuffing them down, which is known to be harmful to our health. Many caregivers and gatekeepers have secret pain or shame that they have not shared with others, swarming around their brains in images and emotions. Through writing, the pain gets translated into black-and-white words that exist outside of ourselves.

24 Developing a suicide safety plan

To intervene in a suicide attempt, a safety plan for the person considering suicide can help. A safety plan is a collaborative and practical tool that helps people at risk identify suicide warning signs, activate coping mechanisms, and seek support during moments of intense distress. Stanley and Brown (2012) found that safety planning emphasises empowerment, connection, and readiness. Having written down and planned a safety plan means it does not have to be developed in the heat of the crisis. A safety plan is not the same as a safety or no-suicide contract. The contract was originally developed by Drye et al. (1973) as a questionnaire called the "no-suicide decision". Throughout the years, the term "no-suicide contract" was used. Suicide-prevention contracts are dependent upon an established physician-patient relationship, and are therefore not recommended for use in emergency settings. A contract also might provide a false sense of security. A person's willingness (or reluctance) to enter into a verbal or written suicide-prevention contract does not guarantee that a suicide attempt will never happen. If such a contract is breached, legal action cannot restore a person's life. Bryan et al. (2017) and Stanley et al. (2012) found that a safety plan is more effective than a safety contract. When a plan is created with a caregiver or a gatekeeper, the safety plan becomes both a personal guide and a shared intervention framework.

So what are the requirements for a safety plan? First of all, it should be written in the person's own words and be easy to read. Secondly, active involvement of the person's support systems, for example, friends or family members, provides clarity in the role they play during a suicide situation. Thirdly, the safety plan should be grounded in trauma-informed and recovery-oriented approaches. This includes not the assumption that families and friends are safe and supportive. Fourthly, the plan should be revisited and collaboratively updated from time to time and during encounters, as circumstances may have changed. Adding and changing items as needed is highly recommended. Finally, the plan should remain in the possession of the person with suicidal thoughts at all times.

Implementing a safety plan is a six-step process. If the first step does not work, the person in crisis can move to the next step in the plan. The first part of the safety plan involves recognising personal warning signs indicating a potential escalation toward suicidal crisis. Stanley et al. (2018) point out that self-awareness regarding warning signs enhances self-regulation and leads to a reduction in impulsive suicidal acts. The central questions a person needs to ask themselves are: *"How will I know when the safety plan should be used?"* and *"What do I experience when I start to think about suicide or feel extremely depressed?"* Warning signs could be mood shifts, images, changes in sleep, behaviours, or thoughts.

The second part is about internal coping strategies. Those are actions that the person in distress can perform without immediate help. When discussing strategies, a collaborative, problem-solving approach helps address potential roadblocks. The questions here the person should ask themselves: *"What can I do, on my own, if I become suicidal again, to help myself not to act on my thoughts or urges?"* A caregiver or gatekeeper can ask them, *"How likely do you think you would be able to do this step during a time of crisis?"* to assess the likelihood of using that strategy. Some coping strategies could be breathing techniques, listening to music, or going for a walk, as long as these actions have been shown to help them reduce the distress they have experienced. Brown and Stanley (2008) found that if this is practised beforehand, it will increase the effectiveness during the suicidal thought or attempt when the cognitive function might be impaired.

The third step is to incorporate social coping strategies into the plan. These strategies focus on social contacts, such as family, friends, or peers, who may be able to distract the person in crisis. In this step, the goal is to move away from suicidal emotions, thoughts, and feelings. Holt-Lunstad et al. (2015) underline that social engagement can reduce feelings of isolation, improve emotional regulation, and interrupt ruminative thinking. Questions to ask are: *"Who or what social settings help you take your mind off your problems at least for a little while?"* or *"Which places can you go to be around people?"*. It is important to have several people and social settings listed so there will be more options in case one of the options is unavailable. When compiling a list, identify potential obstacles and the likelihood that the person in crisis will engage in this step. The fourth step is to identify whom to reach out to, what kind of support they can offer, and how to contact them during a crisis. These people could include, for example, family members, caregivers, friends, colleagues, teachers, or gatekeepers. In this step, unlike the previous one, people reveal to others they trust that they are in crisis. Having a gatekeeper involved makes sure these contacts are realistic, informed, and ready to help when needed. Questions to ask are: *"Who is supportive of you, and whom do you feel that you can talk with when you are under stress?"* and *"How would you prioritise the list of people to contact, in case someone cannot be reached?"*. Sometimes, role-play and rehearsal can be useful at this step. Kleiman and Liu (2013) argue that feeling supported socially can contribute to decreasing the chance of having suicidal thoughts and help prevent the situation from worsening.The fifth step is to identify which professionals or agencies to contact and how. Potential resources could be mental health providers, crisis hotlines, emergency services, and community organisations. Also consider that some resources might not be available 24/7. Questions to ask around this step could be *"What are the mental health professionals that we should identify to be on your safety plan?"* or *"What other health care providers should be considered?"*. Having gatekeepers in place plays a vital role in making professional help feel more normal and in reducing stigma and fear. Stanley et al. (2018) found that plans with specific crisis resources are connected to fewer instances of suicidal behaviour and improved engagement with treatment.The sixth and last step in the suicide safety plan is to make the environment safe. By taking such measures, it can reduce access to harmful methods in case a person considers going over to the extreme of committing suicide. Harmful methods include the use of medications, firearms, sharp objects, and ropes. The Harvard T. H. Chan School of Public Health (2023) underlines that by limiting access to lethal means, the risk of death can be lowered without simply shifting the method used. The questions to be asked could be: *"Do you own a firearm, such as a gun or rifle?"* and *"What other means do you have access to and may use to attempt to kill yourself?"* Stanley and Brown (2012) show that people with higher-quality safety plans are less likely to be hospitalised in the year after safety planning. Having a person with suicidal thoughts write their suicidal safety plan with a gatekeeper acknowledges their autonomy and expertise on what they find helpful. Providers should enter the safety planning process with an open mind and a sense of curiosity, while also drawing on knowledge of support measures that have helped others in the past.

24.1 A Story: The climb

Ziya often found herself pondering over one question: *"Is there really one thing that helps in getting over mental illness? Something that could stop the relapses from creeping back in?"* She always wondered if mental illness was something out of her control, like the support of her friends and family, or something much more intrinsic, like a kind of resilience she had not discovered yet.She asked around, made little surveys that said, *"Hey guys, click on what helped you,"* and the answers came back in shades of greys and blues: my friends helped me, my family supported me, I found it within myself, I got better when I decided I wanted to get better, all you need is time and patience.However, nothing gave her peace. Her friends and family were very helpful. Always available if Ziya needed something. But for some reason, the more they showed up for her, the guiltier she felt for not already feeling better. Ziya tried to find resilience within herself, but all she found was an overwhelming sense of fatigue and exhaustion. Giving up was easier, wasn't it? Patience felt like a cruel joke being played upon her. Two years had already gone by since she had been dealing with her demons in her head. How much longer was she supposed to wait?So one day, she thought, *"Forget it. I will experiment on my own."* She tried everything her doctor suggested, everything she read, therapy, medicines, exercises and six months passed by. Finally, Ziya stumbled upon an answer. Not the kind of answer that fits neatly on a piece of paper or a social media post; it was not very glamorous or inspiring, but it was real and honest, and it helped. The answer was consistency.

Ziya explained it in her own words: "Well, I did all the things people told me to. None of it worked for me unless I kept it consistently. That is when it all came together and started to make sense. Was it easy at the beginning? No, it was definitely very hard. I used to skip medicines, and then I wondered why my brain felt like a derailed rollercoaster. It did not make sense to me. But when I stopped treating the good days like a free pass and stopped saying that one missed dose would not matter, that is when I started seeing results. What works is consistency. Taking medicines consistently, going to therapy consistently, practising all the heavy, difficult, boring grounding exercises consistently. That is what helps."Of course, there were still those days when she slipped, days when she could not keep up with the rhythm. But the moment she could get back to being consistent, she would pick herself up and get back on track. Practical consistency was enough. So what worked for Ziya? It was neither one magical cure nor one heroic burst of strength. Just the steady act of showing up: for your medicines, your therapy, your self-care. Over and over again, until it becomes a habit. A way of living where you do not constantly ruminate but are one with yourself.

25 Family involvement in suicide prevention

An important source in getting a better understanding of the private situation, what might help or does not and how they can support and function as a safety net for a person with suicidal thoughts is family. Family plays a central role in keeping the person safe by reducing access to means of self-harm, for example. Members of the family often notice early changes in the person in crisis's mood, behaviour, and functioning. Changes that could indicate suicidal risk. Turecki et al. (2019) argue that detecting these signs early can prompt immediate action, such as seeking help or intervening. Relationships with family can provide emotional continuity and a sense of belonging. Joiner (2005) notes that these provisions can counter feelings of isolation and burden. These feelings play an important psychological factor in suicide ideation. There are conditions, however. The supportive family needs to be nonjudgmental and emotionally available, according to Kleiman and Liu (2013), to contribute to lowering the suicidal risk. In suicide prevention, the role of the family comes first, as family loves you unconditionally, even though it is hard and painful at times. The suicidal person wants family with them, not necessarily mental health professionals. While there are many advantages to involving family members, there can also be a downside. Family involvement is not without difficulties. Cerel et al. (2008) argue that emotional overload and role strain can impair responses. Family members can experience anxiety, depression or burnout if guilt, fear, or a sense of sole responsibility come into play.

It is also sometimes difficult for family members since they often do not understand the reasons for suicide or do not know what the right response is to it. McMains et al. (2021) note that the family may also be reluctant to help, asking themselves, "What if I mess up and that person dies?" Family dynamics, shaped by how they communicate, may unintentionally worsen distress, particularly when conflicts, enmeshment, or poor boundaries are present. Linehan (1993) shows that responses that minimise feelings or seek to control behaviour can increase shame and withdrawal, thereby raising the risk of considering suicide rather than reducing it. Unfortunately, silence and secrecy within the family environment have also sometimes prevented family members from intervening to potentially change the course of suicide intent. If a family is unwilling to disclose the context of the secrecy, it may make it more difficult to understand what is going on, which can result in not receiving the proper support from a caregiver or gatekeeper. For a person with suicidal thoughts, it can also trigger fears of disappointing family, of being judged, or of losing independence, which may cause individuals to hide their struggles, especially in stigmatising environments, according to Hom et al. (2017). Overall, the most effective family involvement in suicide prevention is supportive, collaborative, and supplemented by professional guidance. Families can be strong allies, but should not replace trained mental health care professionals. Timely intervention may be effective before the person chooses the last option.

25.1 The audience effect

So many people, so many opinions. The audience effect, also known as social facilitation, is described by Triplett (1898) as a psychological event in which a person's thoughts, feelings, or actions can change simply because others are present, whether they are actually present or only perceived. Zajonc (1966) argues that this idea helps explain why people might perform differently, regulate themselves, or make different decisions when they know they are being watched or judged. When it comes to distress and suicidal behaviour, the audience effect can be pretty complex. Sometimes having family members or friends at hand can be a comforting presence. Hawton and Williams (2001) found that knowing that others are close and paying attention can make it less likely that someone will act on suicidal thoughts during a crisis. Even though opinions and advice might be well-meaning, they can also add pressure. People with suicidal thoughts might feel the urge to hide their distress, pretending they are doing well. The problem is that, as Baumeister and Leary (1995) note, when they feel they must appear strong rather than show vulnerability, this can trigger or intensify feelings of self-consciousness, deepening inner struggles and emotional exhaustion. For families and friends, the audience effect heightens feelings of duty, shame, or fear of being judged. This shows that the presence of others is not always helpful; how it influences someone depends a lot on the quality of relationships, open communication, and emotional safety.

25.2 A Story: Never let me down

Abandonment is a very strange word. It weighs heavily on everyone who recognises it, yet often misuses it. People fear being abandoned, yet, ironically, they abandon their own loved ones, sometimes knowingly, sometimes at the very moment they are needed most. Abandonment often happens in two steps. First comes quiet emotional abandonment, followed by sudden physical abandonment. Emotional withdrawal arrives softly. It almost feels like a sunset, the light fading along with it. It is most resisted, and when efforts to prevent it fail, all that remains is the physical presence of a loved one who is no longer emotionally present. However, people cling to this last trace of presence, trying to delay the inevitable.Nick understands this fear. He knows it in his bones and blood. Abandonment has been a constant fear in his life. It probably began in childhood, when his parents' anger and arguments took the form of threats to leave. His mother would often storm out, warning that she would never return, leaving Nick in tears, wondering if she ever would. Her words would sting him: *"You will understand when I am not around."* These are awful words to use in front of a child, and Nick was no exception. They made space in his mind. He began to associate being left behind with the most painful form of punishment, the kind he learned to believe he deserved.

The cycle did not end at home. It followed him to school. His friends, knowingly or unknowingly, manifested the same fear. If Nick did not act in accordance with their expectations, they would threaten to cut ties with him, leaving him rejected and alone. Over time, he internalised this pattern. Nick began mirroring the same behaviour he feared. He used threats of leaving to express his frustration. Starting to pack his bags multiple times, hoping his mother would notice and stop him, hoping she would understand the depth of his struggle. If nothing else worked, perhaps the idea that Nick was willing to leave home would finally make his loved ones love him better, cherish him more.

What began as fear started manifesting ironically as Nick grew older. He began asking others to leave him before they could abandon him themselves. It was a defence mechanism born from years of emotional pain and perceived abandonment. Beneath the surface of an emotionally cold person lived a deeply fragile man, whose trauma was shaped and later compounded by a diagnosis of depression.

Nick was never physically abandoned by his parents. They were always there, physically. He could count on their presence. However, whether they were emotionally available is a different story altogether. Nick often called it a generational gap. He was born in the 90s, a time when parenting relied heavily on fear, threats, and scolding. It was his parents' limitations; their inability to learn emotional availability because of their age, beliefs, and simply not knowing how. Their intentions were good, but not enough to bridge the gap between them and Nick.

The pain of emotional abandonment is tailor-made for every person. It is easy to promise never to abandon loved ones, but most people mean only physical presence. Emotional abandonment, though less visible, can be far more damaging. It leaves a person feeling unseen, unheard, and painfully alone. It is also difficult to explain this kind of pain. How do you say: *"I know you are here, sitting right in front of me, but I feel invisible. I have been unhappy for so long, yet I cannot share it with you because you are not really here for me, not emotionally. I miss you, even though you are right here."*

Nick's fear of abandonment carried into his adult relationships. He lost friends and grew increasingly sceptical of forming connections. Those who stayed were often present only physically, leaving him suffocated by their half-presence. However, Nick was terrified to let go. He was too fragile to carry the weight of another failed connection, so he did what he knew. He clung to relationships that drained him, because even suffocation felt better than abandonment again.

It is important to understand that abandonment does not always arrive with a goodbye or a closed door. Sometimes it begins as a quiet withdrawal of care and understanding. It is the absence of being seen, the loss of a place to rest your emotions. This kind of abandonment lingers, leaving scars that even time struggles to heal.

Most often, abandonment manifests as emotional unavailability. Nick remembers an incident from college, when he was living far from home for his studies. One day, he came down with severe food poisoning. He called his family, but they lived far away and could not reach him in time. He turned to his friends, but they were busy and unavailable. Even his flatmates were occupied with exams. Left with no choice, Nick managed alone; he visited the doctor by himself and got through the day. By evening, dehydration caused him to faint. That was when people in his building came to his aid. His friends arrived later to help him get stitches for the injuries he sustained from the fall. One of them asked, "Why didn't you tell me your food poisoning was this serious? I would

have come in the morning." Nick could only think of how he had already reached out earlier, only to be met with dismissive responses like, "Take care, you will be fine." The experience left deep emotional scars.
After extensive therapy, Nick admits the trauma remains. It shows up in adulthood now that he lives alone for work. Despite twelve-hour workdays, there are times when he finds himself unbearably lonely. Coming home to an empty apartment, he yearns for someone to talk to, but people are rarely available. He understands he cannot force anyone to be there for him, yet that understanding does nothing to ease the crushing pain of isolation.

One incident stays vivid in his mind. He had been seeing a woman at the time, and one evening he called her. He asked if she could see him or invite him over,if they could just sit together somewhere. Her mother was unwell, and she could not leave the house. Nick struggled with a familiar feeling of abandonment. His scars made him notice subtle shifts in availability. Intellectually, he understood why she could not come that night. But for someone carrying deep emotional wounds, even a slight change in attention feels like salt on an unhealed wound. It stings.

This woman, who once spent hours with him despite countless responsibilities, seemed less available lately. That night, he could not help but wonder: What is the point of having people in your life who claim to love you if they cannot be there when you need them? It is easy to stay during good times. Even in bad times, people often show up initially; but eventually, emotional withdrawal begins, followed by physical distance that only widens with time.

Overwhelmed by the weight of his feelings, Nick did something he is not proud of. He tried to drink a corrosive substance. It is hard to say why. Perhaps he believed this was how life would always be:a cycle of abandonment at his most vulnerable moments. Perhaps he felt disconnected from a world where people seemed comfortable neglecting their loved ones. Alternatively, perhaps it was a desperate attempt to be seen, a cry for someone to notice his pain.

Physical pain, after all, is easier to understand than emotional pain. Nevertheless, the irony is that actions meant to signal distress often drive people away. Nick's girlfriend was terrified. She assured him, "I am not leaving you." However, the damage was already done. Nick felt more emotionally distant and more abandoned than ever before. Nick says it has been more than a year since he heard from her.

25.3 A Story: Listen

Casie fractured her leg a few months back. The painful ordeal left her bedridden for around three or four months. Those months were very challenging for her, both physically and emotionally. Casie wanted to heal. She made sure that she took all her medicines, never missed her supplements, and did not skip doctor's appointments. Still, healing takes time. A fracture takes time to heal, no matter how disciplined one is.

During this time, she needed more than just medical care. Obviously, she needed some support. She reached out to her roommates, with whom she was living at the time, and asked for specific help with her daily struggles. She asked if they could help her get out of bed and back into it because she was unable to do it by herself, given her fractured ankle and leg.

Her friends did not say yes to that. Instead, they had another offer for her. They volunteered to feed her, saying they would feed her with their hands since she could use her arms and hands very well. Their intentions were pure, and they genuinely wanted to help, so she could not say anything, even though this was not what she wanted help with. Now, Casie continued to struggle. She asked again if they could help her sit in a wheelchair so she could move more easily. They offered to pay for her meals instead, insisting it was their way of helping her with the burden since she was unable to work. Their intentions were good, but this was not what she needed.

Every day, her struggles continued. When she asked for another favour, if they could keep a table with her medicines and other essentials within reach so she would not have to get out of bed, they instead offered to rearrange the tables to make things more organised and easier to grab once she reached the table. Their hearts were in the right place, but their actions were not really helping.

Finally, Casie mustered the courage and asked for some time and patience as she recovered, because healing a broken bone takes time. One of her roommates suggested that she should visit the doctor more often to speed up the healing process. While it makes sense to visit the doctor on time, do frequent visits speed up that natural healing process? A bone takes time to attach itself.

It is easy to wonder what went wrong. Her friends were kind-hearted. They wanted to help, and they did help in their own way. They offered to feed her, they offered to pay for her meals, and they offered to arrange a table. Nevertheless, she did not need help with her arms, finances, or organisational skills. She needed help with her fractured leg. Therefore, it seems a little weird.

This kind of mismatch happens very rarely in physical illness. People are generally very quick to offer specific, meaningful support. They understand what a person needs and try to adapt accordingly.

Now, if you change fracture to invisible depression, Casie had depression and could not leave her room for days, with an overwhelming sense of tiredness and loneliness. She was talking to a therapist and taking medication, but getting out of depression takes time. She reached out to her loved ones for support. She requested a roommate to spend more time with her so she would not feel alone. Her roommate, with the best of intentions, instead hoped to cheer her up by asking her family to sit with her.

Casie pleaded for patience. She knew she was not going to recover overnight and that recovery would need time and understanding from everyone around her. Instead, friends and family urged her to see her therapist more frequently, as if that alone would replace the empathy and support she desperately needed from them.

This is the reality of mental illness. People always want to help, but often in ways that are convenient for them, and those ways may not actually be truly meaningful to the person they are helping. Intentions are good, but not enough.

It is like a child crying out for food, only to be given a blanket instead. The gesture is kind, but it does nothing to fulfil the child's hunger. This is what getting help with mental illness often feels like. The help offered very rarely aligns with what is truly needed. While good intentions are definitely applauded by the world and even by the person on the receiving end, the person is still unheard, unseen, and unsupported.

True support is not always about good intentions or convenience. It is about listening, understanding, and offering what a person truly needs. It lies in asking what the person needs and, if it is within one's capacity, helping with that, even if it is hard. Healing, whether physical or emotional, requires not just effort. It also requires the right amount of empathy: not so much that it overwhelms the caregiver, but not so little that it serves no purpose to the person dealing with illness.

26 The farewell

When a person says goodbye, either by phone, text, or a suicide note, before a suicide attempt, the impact can be intense and may last for a long time. This is not only for those who are on the verge of committing suicide, but for family, friends, the caregiver, or gatekeeper who hears it too. Joiner (2005) notes that such farewells have a direct link with increased risk of suicide, as people wanting to commit suicide believe that the future will no longer bring something positive for them.

At first, it might sound innocent from them. Maybe making fun of it, sometimes using cryptic messages or metaphors. It may even be that they are literally describing their chosen method. Malone & McGuinness (2009) found that 80% of people who took their own lives had previously talked about it. Unfortunately, often the people around the person in crisis do not listen to what the person on the verge of life and death is trying to say, downplaying the message and contributing to an even deeper crisis.

For the person attempting suicide, saying goodbye often reflects psychological pain that is too overwhelming for them to bear. It can also indicate that they have given up all hope and perceive that their life is nearing its end. Saying goodbye verbally can indicate that there might be still some doubt in their mind about pursuing the act of attempting suicide. That small opportunity might leave room to intervene and connect with a person in despair. However, it can also be seen as an attempt to reduce the emotional burden on loved ones or the people who took care of them, and as an indication that they are ok with their choice. From their perspective, they think they are bringing relief to their family because finally, someone so worthless and hopeless will no longer bother them.

Caregivers and gatekeepers should be aware that hearing a goodbye from them might trigger feelings of guilt or helplessness. Those feelings will be even stronger when the outcome is unknown or tragic. Even when a suicide attempt is survived, the emotional weight of having heard a potential final message can persist and affect professional confidence and well-being.

26.1 Understanding suicide notes

Suicide notes themselves, when they exist, offer a highly personal look into the inner world of someone who is experiencing profound psychological pain. They are not logical explanations, nor are they clear roadmaps intended for understanding why a person reached the point they did. Instead, suicide notes tend to reflect emotional moods, beliefs about the self, and perceptions of the world at a moment when suffering appears overwhelming and inescapable.

Ramsland (2012) found that in a lot of suicide notes, there is a clear sense of not belonging coming back as a common theme. Disconnection can be expressed in sentences such as *"I cannot find my place in life," "I do not feel part of any group,"* or *"I am lonely"*. It may also suggest that our world can easily exist without them. For the person writing the note, this sense of displacement can feel permanent and defining. Those feelings often develop over time and may be reinforced by repeated experiences of rejection, failure, or internal self-criticism.

Strongly connected to the theme of disconnection, another common theme can be found: the belief that suicide will somehow reduce the burden on family or friends. *"This is the best for everyone"*, or *"I will no longer bother you"*, found in suicide notes underline such a belief. It highlights how severely a person's self-worth and self-esteem have eroded. Those feelings stem originally from intense guilt or shame. The person attempting suicide also has a distorted, although sincere, perception that their existence causes harm, inconvenience, or pain to loved ones.

Another commonality theme is ambivalence. Many people who contemplate suicide do not want to die. They want the pain to stop and see that ending their life is the only remaining option. This can be expressed through disclosures such as: *"I do not want to go, but there is nothing else that anyone can do"*.

Self-criticism and internal chaos are another recurring theme. Expressions like *"I have never been much good"* or *"I am all twisted up inside"* reveal harsh self-judgment and confusion about the person's identity and emotions. Long periods of internal struggle, mental health challenges and emotional instability are reflected in these statements.

The last important theme, which is often addressed in suicide notes, is the request for forgiveness or mercy. Enright et al. (1998) define forgiveness as: “a willingness to abandon one’s right to resentment, negative judgment, and indifferent behaviour toward one who unjustly injured us, while fostering the undeserved qualities of compassion, generosity, and even love toward him or her.”

Asking for forgiveness can be a way of acknowledging the harm their actions and consequences will cause to their family, friends, and loved ones. It reflects the guilt that they feel and the social stigma about suicide. Suicide notes often begin or end with a note of forgiveness to highlight its importance and are meant to be delivered to the recipient or recipients after they have died. The writer also seeks moral closure by asking for it.

Mercy can be defined as: ” the disposition to alleviate another’s suffering or to refrain from punishment, even when justice would permit or demand it.” (Aquinas, 1981)

Phrases that invoke mercy or ask for divine compassion reflect the cultural and spiritual frameworks of the writers, where suicide is seen in the context of moral judgment and grace.

A famous Dutch singer, Herman Brood, wrote a suicide note to his wife and kids before he jumped off the rooftop of the Hilton in Amsterdam. The note was handed to one of the barkeepers at the Hilton, right before he went to the rooftop. The note was published in De Telegraaf with his wife’s permission after his death on July 11,

2001. Her reason was that it was good for the public to know that he was not under the influence of anything and that his act was planned. The last sentence, "drown in my own tears", shows, according to his wife, that he was depressed and felt hopelessness because he would be leaving his wife and kids behind.

Below, you will find his suicide note translated into English:

> XANDRA AND ALL HONEYS
>
> This speed, instead of burning out, I will leave that to the cremation.
>
> My last wish: "Continue as I did with Grieg, B.I.G. and Lou and do not be sad. Celebrate it.
>
> One day I will see you again. I will go bungee jumping now without a cord.
>
> Mercy - pappa
>
> DROWN IN MY OWN TEARS

26.2 The day I tried to live: a suicide note.

In one of the conversations with people who attempted to commit suicide, one of the people was willing to share their suicide note. "I can not believe that this was actually me who wrote this. I am in a much happier place now and glad that the attempt failed", the person said. This note contains actual suicidal thinking, planning language, and emotional finality.

I do not know what is happening. I feel something very heavy on my chest, inside my throat, and on my eyes. The tears are burning as they trickle down my face onto my neck. They burn the path they make down. It feels like I will feel like this forever, like it is the end of the world, like even if it gets better, it will again go worse.

I feel like I am way too much for everyone, for my parents, who have been trying to get me out of this. I come out of this momentarily, and then I fall back deeper, and they grow ten years older in the span of a week. It would be better to just end it all, like for once, at least I would not be the reason for this consistent pain. They will be sad, but at least they will not be disappointed again and again, like I have been giving them hope and then taking it back in the worst way possible.

I feel so ashamed to be alive, like I am crying over things that should not matter, and yet I cannot stop them from mattering. I know there are other things I could put my energy into, but for some reason, everything is triggering: every short phone call, every missed call, everyone I want to talk to not picking up, every late reply. It is not supposed to feel this way. Am I the only one who does not understand what is happening?

It is like I am not meant for this world, like I am someone who would never fit, like people like me should not exist. They are not meant for this world. I can barely breathe right now. I can physically feel the pain in my heart. I wish I could die naturally. I should have, by the way, I have not been eating or doing anything to make my brain or heart happy, but nothing is helping. Maybe I need to take matters into my own hands. Should I do it?

What would happen to my parents? They are the only people who seem to care, yet I am not able to stay even for them. Staying, making myself suffer for someone else, is not happiness. I do not want to suffer anymore. This is getting difficult. I tried so hard. I am taking my medicines. My therapy. Talking to people. However, eventually, I end up messing everything up, and it does not stop.

I am sure that even if it stops, it will come back, and I am not ready for me to get better only to fall back into it all over again. If this is what life is going to be about,a small high after a big low, and then another high preparing for a bigger low, I am not willing to do it. It is my life. It is my death. It is supposed to be right.

I feel like I am not doing the life thing right. You know, the people I have talked to seem to have it worked out, even if things are not working for them. It is like their problems are still somehow more interesting than me, that they are able to talk it out, or they just know how to keep it all inside them, and I am unable to.

Maybe humans are not supposed to talk about what is bothering them, and since I am someone who cannot talk about things, I cannot survive. I do not want to live in a world with people who cannot even talk about what is going on in their heads. I mean, what is the point? I have seen people giving great speeches, talking about things for hours, but when it comes to talking about how they are feeling or listening to what others are feeling, people seem to run away. I actually hate this word and all the people in it. I do not wish to be part of this world anymore.

And I feel like I have made everyone run away. Like I have called my friends multiple times crying, and I do not even know what the reason is that I am crying. Just anything triggers me. Like, this person did not say hi as he used to, okay, I am triggered. Why? I am not even a good friend with this person.

What is happening inside? Is this brain going to be like this for the rest of my life? Is it bound to happen after every good phase? I cannot have this. I literally cannot have this.

I want to really apologise to mamma and papa. I love you. I know you are the only people who love me and care for me. Moreover, I know that after I am gone, you will have to listen to society and its theories about what might have led to this. There will be an open investigation. It is weird that I am more scared of an investigation into my own life. One thing that might stop me is not wanting to put my parents and friends through a legal investigation.

Suicide is not a natural death. It will be looked into, and then society will have its theories that maybe she did it for a guy. It is always that. The first time I got this episode, I was asked if this was about a guy. The second time it happened again, if this was another guy. I cannot pinpoint one person. It just happens. Something, and everything seems to set me off.

But I want to assure mamma and papa that it is not about a guy. It is just that I am not able to do it any longer. I tried. I genuinely tried. I tried all this, but again I am back into this, and even after trying everything, I am falling back into this. I do not want to do it again. It has been a rollercoaster, and I do not want to continue any longer.

I googled painless ways to die. I think death is not supposed to be painless, or I do not know. Maybe I will go soon. But I want to shout at the top of my lungs, scream so loud. I just want life to leave me in that moment, but that will not happen.

I am just looking at things, like my hands are shaking. My face looks so red and tired. Like, I do not think there is anything to look forward to. Harming myself little by little helps me take my mind off the mental pain, but eventually it comes back. So this is the time. I end all.

I am sorry. Mamma Papa, I really love you, but I am not able to do it anymore. I do not know what will happen after this, but I genuinely pray for you guys to be happy and learn to live without me, which will be difficult. I know that. But could you please understand;you want me to be happy. I think this is how I will be happy. You are supposed to be happy in my happiness.

I am sorry. I could not do it any longer.

This suicide note shows an acute depressive episode with: Intense hopelessness ("It will always come back."), perceived burdensomeness ("I am way too much for everyone."), shame-based identity collapse ("I feel ashamed to be alive."), suicidal ideation with rumination and planning language. It shows someone who is exhausted and cornered, given the situation they are in. One can also notice several cognitive distortions, such as fortune-telling, mind-reading, all-or-nothing thinking, and personalisation.

The person shifts from feeling pain to believing they should not exist, which suggests a profound identity-level collapse. The text's tone is not chaotic; it is structured. The note moves from physical sensation to relational guilt, existential rejection, justification and ends with an apology. While going between despair and logic, the text still indicates that cognitive capacity remains intact despite emotional overwhelm. This note reveals that the person does not necessarily want to die but wants to stop the cycle, shame, the burden feeling, the relapse pattern and unpredictability. Death is framed as escape from recurrence, not from life itself. One of the most important lines in the note is "If even after trying everything I am to fall back into this, I do not want to do it again." This reflects exhaustion, not apathy. Exhaustion can feel permanent, while it is not.

It is important to understand that suicide notes are not always coherent, complete, or representative of a person's entire life or identity. They are written from a place of acute distress, narrowed thinking, and emotional overload. What they consistently communicate is not a clear rationale for death, but the depth of suffering the person was experiencing at that moment. Suicide notes can trigger intense emotions and unanswered questions. The following quote of a family member of a person underlines this: *"I find it incredibly hard, even traumatic, that nobody in our family got a chance to say goodbye or I love you."* While they may offer some insight into the person's pain, they should never be interpreted as proof that suicide was inevitable or that family, friends, caregivers, gatekeepers, or others failed.

27 A conversation about suicide: erase and rewind

One of the authors of this book, Pascal Comvalius, had the opportunity to get back in contact with Joni Parker, a twenty-six-year-old woman from Chanhassen, MN, USA, who had considered and had failed attempts at committing suicide for a long time. Pascal acted twice as a suicide prevention gatekeeper during her last two attempts. Our conversation was so important that we felt compelled to share it with you in full.

Take us back, what was the first time you started to ideate suicide?

Well, I think it was already there when I was a child. I used to think that maybe I had been loved or valued more if I were not here. That if something were to happen to me, people would be relieved. But it never actually materialised until 2020. The thought was always at the back of my head that if something were to happen to me, people around me would feel better, and maybe they would understand me because I am not able to put across what I am otherwise. But in 2020, when I think about it now, because of the pandemic, we were limited in our freedom, and I got a lot of time to introspect, and I think I just skipped it. I just jumped ahead and thought that's it. Not that I did not like the way my life was, I just thought about it way too much, and I thought, okay, there is no point, just end it. It started in 2020 and lasted for years.

Was it already right at the start of COVID?

COVID has already been gone for a year, or is it just? It is very ironic because I was actually having the time of my life just when COVID started. I was travelling, I was going out. That all changed when COVID started, and I felt I was losing out on what was actually good in my life. And I thought maybe this is my destiny, that even if I get something good, it will go away. Therefore, there is no point in trying to live. So I remember precisely that it was December 2020 when it started happening for the first time, when I harmed myself. And then it was a long journey.

Moreover, what do you mean by harming yourself? What do I have to think about?

I used to cut myself on my arm with anything, any object I could see.

Ok, it is my understanding that gradually over time it has become worse or more frequent, or how do I have to see that?

Yes, the first time I did it, I thought, Okay, it is done. Then I will not do it again. But something would make me go there again, the dark space. And I would do it again and again. I even took help in December 2020 itself. I found an online therapist and everything to talk about this, but maybe my research was not good enough, or the therapist was not good enough. It did not help. So I thought, it is winter, we used to wear long sleeves. The marks on my arms are not visible to anyone, not even to my parents. This actually helped me do it more often, as I was convinced there was nothing to hold me back.

And at that time, you were also living with your parents, right?

Yes, I was living with my parents because of COVID-19. Colleges were closed, and I was stuck at home.

So help me understand how you were able to hide that from your parents. Or could you even hide it?

Firstly, they never expected that something like this would happen. Just under their nose, like inside our house. So they never checked. Secondly, I was very good at hiding the cuts and scars on my arms. Besides that, I have a very smiley face. Many times, I have been told by multiple people, "Oh, you have a nice smile, and I can smile through anything." I will be having the worst day of my life, and I can just smile through it. So I think they never thought that this would happen. But even during sleep or when I was out, I was very careful, especially when I was with friends and family, but I had to be even more careful when I was home. I had to wear longer sleeves. I had to; even when the weather started to change towards Spring and Summer, I was still wearing long sleeves until the marks faded. But I think this was never suspected because there was no reason for them to suspect that anything was happening.

And you have done multiple attempts, right?

Yes, a lot. Four or five, I think.

Four or five, okay, and were these attempts, if you still remember, always in one place, such as home?

Thankfully, it is an easy memory now. My first attempt, I was home alone, I was uh it was again covered, and I just took a lot of pills, and I did not know what those pills did, but I thought they would do something, and maybe I would not wake up or something that was home. The second time, I think it was where I was living and studying. I was not feeling well, so I did the same thing again. The third time was when I was working. I was living in a separate place in Apple Valley, Minnesota, and I think it actually escalated over time. Then the last time I remember, I was home, and again, it came back to where it started the last time it happened. Different cases, different triggers, all that, and I found myself wanting to end my life by suicide again.

Okay. You are also talking about different methods for doing it, right? First, you have tried to cut yourself. Next to that, you were also just talking about taking just an overdose of pills.

I think I never cut myself to kill myself. For that, I knew that was not actually very possible. I thought about it, but I did some research. Instead, I took the pills. After that did not work, it escalated to drinking some corrosive substances. I am still appalled at how I am still alive after all the things I have done. And then last, I remember, I hung myself from a fan. That was the last attempt I remember.

Yeah. I remember, because it was a day before I was going back to the USA. You called me and asked, " Hey, how are you? And I answered, "Yeah, I am fine. How are you?" And you said, "Oh, I am also fine." That is when I said, "No, you're not, I will not disconnect the phone until I am sure that you are safe." Furthermore, we were, for an hour and a half, on the phone. It was 10.30 pm.

Yes, it was late at night. I remember that. I was sitting on the sofa right in front of you, just crying and talking to you. I told you that I just tried to hang myself. The attempt failed since I messed up the knot and disfigured the fan blades. That is also how my parents found out: the next morning, they said to me that it looked like something had happened here. They took me to the hospital the next day, where I spent an entire day with a mental health professional.

So, it went from cutting yourself, to taking pills, to drinking gross stuff, to hanging. If you were to talk in terms of chances of surviving a suicide attempt, hanging is the most lethal of all of them. Luckily, the hanging failed. Talked about cycling back to the gross substances you drank, what kind of things do I have to think of?

Well, it started when I used to overdose on cough medicines because they would not help me sleep. I used to do that initially, but eventually, they would only make you sleep for a day or two. And then you would be fine because that is all they could do. So I went on to other liquids. I tried to drink a Dettol anti-disinfectant hand soap once, but could not swallow it. The second time, I tried to drink Harpic, the toilet cleaner. I burned my lips with that. Could not ingest it. I remember putting it in my mouth, but I could not swallow it. Just puked it out with the effect that it burned my lips and my tongue. But hey, look at me, after all these attempts, I am still smiling. The difference is that it is a genuine smile.

Which is great, look at the result. We are having a conversation about a sensitive topic while still joking around. You are out of that awful period in your life, so... That is a good thing. But during those times, right after you make these attempts, what goes through your mind? Are there things that you think about? What do you recall?

Those times were different at all times. The first time I was, I do not remember exactly because there were a lot of thoughts, and I still had not learned to make sense of them. I just knew I was feeling something, and I wanted to stop feeling it. And then I remembered I would feel useless, like everyone was going ahead. Everyone seems to be working just fine, and I could not do that. I felt like a misfit, as if I was not meant to be here, and did not feel like an XYZ person. In general, I did not feel like the 99% of people around me. In fact, I think 100% at that point in time, because it was very difficult to find someone who is very open about their struggles. So I used to think that everything was fine, and then I used to think that my struggles were not very substantial. I have friends who have gone through things like they have gone through the loss of their parents or something has happened in the house. I have had, and still have, a very good, fulfilling life. I had my parents, who loved me. I am a single child, so I did not even have to share that love with anyone else. And I was doing fine in college, with good grades, and I could not make sense of it. And I thought maybe this is how I would feel for the rest of my life. So I was like, just end it. I do not want to feel this way. There is no reason I should feel this way, but I do. And I need to stop this. And the second and third times it happened, life was still good because I actually got better between attempts. And then it happened again. And I was like, what is the point if this keeps happening again and again? I cannot redo the process again and again. I do not want to be trapped in that downward spiral, and I do not want to keep crawling out of it. I simply stopped it.

Since the last suicide attempt, the last time we spoke or when you called me up, you changed something in your life. What was it? Was it seeking more mental help, or what was it? What was the breakthrough for you?

I think I became more consistent with what was initially helping me. When I used to feel a little better, I would just think, okay, I do not need help anymore; I will be fine. I realised there were certain patterns I needed to break to avoid falling back into that hole again. It sounds strange, but thankfully, I got physically injured a lot of times after the last attempt. This gave me the opportunity to sit with myself and think. Every time I would get injured, I would think about what was happening in my life. And being more consistent with my medication, with my therapy sessions, that is what got me to break out of it. And I actually think I made my circle very substantial, but small. I stopped caring about a lot of things and just became a little more selfish. It helped. Sometimes it is good to focus on yourself.

So if you look back at that awful period, your parents must have also gone through hell with you, right?

I remember my mother ageing 10 years in 10 days. I could see the wrinkles on her face. It is an image engraved in my mind, and I still think of that. That was around, I believe my third attempt, I was not at my family's house. I was back in college, living somewhere else. My friends called my parents to say something had happened, without telling them anything else. My friends did not tell me why my parents were coming. They just told me they are coming to just meet me since it has been a while. And then I saw my mother, she did not look fine. She looked way too old for her age. She was not this old when I last saw her, just a month ago. And then she told me everything. And I was just so sad. I thought that I had made my parents grow old before they actually, you know, should have. But then, when I got better, I could actually see my mother getting younger again. Before that, I did not even know you could see it in a person's face until I saw it in my mother's. That is when I thought, this impacts them way too much. I saw that happening. This also kept me from continuing my life and being happy. The most beautiful thing is that my mother has a nice glow on her cheeks right now; it is back, and I am very happy about that.

28 Analysis paralysis

Kurien et al. (2014) define this thought-processing behaviour as the tendency to over-analyse a situation or overthink possible outcomes to the point that no decision or action is ultimately taken, resulting in paralysis. Analysis paralysis is not the same as rumination, even though they might sound similar. The difference is that the first one is overthinking to avoid decision-making, and is present- or future-related. The latter is overthinking without moving on and is past-oriented. Analysis paralysis can happen to anyone. In the context of suicide, it can happen to the person considering or attempting suicide and to the caregiver or gatekeeper. Overwhelming fear, psyche-ache or conflicting thoughts can cause the brain to freeze. There might be many options generated, but choosing one to take the next step might feel like an impossible task. This might also decrease their window of tolerance and create space for even more overwhelming thoughts or feelings, leading to a downward spiral.

Caregivers and gatekeepers, on the other hand, might be paralysed by the fear of making the wrong decision or feeling the weight of responsibility. This could result in becoming stuck with oneself, engaging in an internal dialogue rather than focusing on creating safety for the person in crisis. In such a case, it is recommended to immediately seek help from your peers, not only to save the person in need but yourself as well.

29 Surviving suicide, what is next?

The road to recovery and to prevent a person from considering suicide as the only solution is long and faced with difficulties. People who survive a suicidal attempt commonly face psychological and social challenges, including stigma and persistent mental-health difficulties. Understanding recovery is critical for both clinical treatment and suicide prevention. Subramanian et al. (2021) found that people who have attempted suicide are at significantly higher risk of future attempts, particularly during the first years after the initial crisis. Consequently, identifying factors that support recovery and recovery capacity is necessary to reduce the chance of the person attempting to commit suicide again and improve their overall quality of life. Leaving suicidal thoughts behind requires a different approach in recovery as opposed to other psychiatric symptoms. It has been noted that it frequently involves identity reconstruction and the development of new coping strategies. They also point out that changing the global beliefs, values and goals following a period of distress and suicide attempts is necessary to reduce that distress and restore their feeling of purpose. Survivors frequently describe recovery as a gradual process in which they regain control over their lives and make decisions. Unfortunately, the path, as mentioned earlier, is not that straightforward. People may experience periods of stability and being able to enjoy life, followed by episodes of vulnerability or relapse. These fluctuations reflect the complex interactions among psychological instability, environmental stressors, and underlying neurobiological processes.

The road to recovery requires continuous supportive relationships, therapeutic treatments, and internal cognitive changes. Rapid advances in neuroscience have begun to clarify how the brain works, including the underlying networks involved in suicidality and emotion regulation. This will create a path to personalised guidance on effectively dealing with these thoughts. At the same time, it is found that psychotherapy remains one of the most effective tools for reducing suicidal behaviour and supporting recovery. There is still a need to do further research on the long-term consequences of survivors of suicide attempts. In addition, it is equally important to examine other protective factors that promote resilience. Investing in recovery and life reconstruction, mental health practitioners can support the people who are trying to leave the suicidal crisis behind and provide them with a better future. One thing is for sure: a mix of support from loved ones and mental health professionals is crucial to move away from ideating suicide.

29.1 A Story: This is me trying

Kenny used to spend this time reading the words of people who, like him, struggled with the weight of depression and other similar silent battles. Reading felt like a world. He had discovered a place where his loneliness would go away for a while, just a little. It was comforting knowing that there were other people out there who felt the same, who shared the same experiences and similar pains. He would also read stories of people who reached small milestones as they came out of their illness. What caught his attention was that many of those things seemed odd, but they helped people navigate out of their despair very well.

For example, there was a woman who had been struggling with depression and anxiety. She would sometimes be out of its grasp, but every so often she would be pulled under again, sometimes by the change of seasons, for example, when the winter chills set in. However, she had learned to recognise her triggers and patterns. She had already warned her loved ones by saying, "Could you be patient with me during these times?" It was her own way of dealing with things. Her strength lay in knowing what would trigger her and when it would trigger her. It was the silver lining in her mental illness, as well as the calm before the storm. Just knowing when it would hit really helped her navigate her way out of the situation or prevent irreversible damage.

Then he came across another person who found his peace in religion, in God. That person found himself connected to something greater and felt more peaceful knowing that someone was watching over him. This also gave the person the zeal to live with purpose, because that is what religion says. That feeling of connection and purpose was the life jacket in a drowning boat.

There was one particular story that stayed with Kenny. It was a very simple story of a woman. This girl shared her simple victory. She had written, *"I did my dishes today."* The way she wrote it, it seemed she was very proud of it. She was proud that she did her dishes without anxiety, without the heaviness of depression weighing her down. It might seem very small to someone on the outside, who does not know what is going on inside her, but it was an achievement she wanted to share and celebrate, and she did. This made Kenny feel envious. It must be very beautiful to accomplish something so simple without depression weighing over every breath and every action. He strove to achieve something similar someday.

He shared his longing for a similar "victory" with his friend Seb. He said, *"Imagine doing dishes without depression, making it feel like an impossible task."* This made Seb laugh. He called him cute, but he knew deep down. He knew the simplicity of the peace one feels while doing the simplest task. It could give him time to wash away his worries, one dish at a time.

Now, Kenny could not understand what was so cute about doing dishes. To him, it was a miracle, a mundane victory that others might take for granted. But for someone like Kenny, who carried a heavy weight every single day, doing the dishes was like getting something off his chest one dish at a time.

Kenny was weighed down by some things that were very normal and natural for other people. For example, getting out of bed was a battle- a big one. Some days, he had to convince himself to hold his toothbrush, that very heavy toothbrush, and go through the process of spending two minutes on himself, brushing his teeth. It was no simple task to brush one's teeth. It was so much to bear for Kenny and for many others like him. Just the thought of it felt like he was carrying the weight of the world, pressing down on his chest.

There were days when he would feel better. He could get out of bed on those days. However, there were days when it felt like some invisible demon was holding him captive inside his own bed- his body and mind too tired and too weighed down by whatever was going on inside his brain because of his depression and anxiety, which decided to show up deeper on a particular day.

For Kenny, depression was not just an illness. It was what made life seem impossible to live or survive. He accepted the darkness, made peace with it, even found a strange comfort in it. What made him more restless was that his anxiety could come knocking at the door any day. On the days he was already weighed down by depression and wanting to rest, his anxiety would show up, sneak up on him, making it impossible for him to rest. His thoughts raced inside his brain. While depression made it difficult for him to take every step, anxiety made him worry about how not taking any step would impact his life, his career, and how he would crumble under the weight of what could not be seen or helped.

Kenny thought about Seb, his closest friend, and the complexity of struggles. Maybe Seb was one of the privileged ones, one of the few people untouched by the constant battle that Kenny fought every day, every moment, in his brain. Kenny convinced himself that Seb's problems were more real, more tangible. He had issues with his wife, struggles at work, but these issues were external. They could be seen. They could be explained better. Moreover, since they could be explained better, they could be resolved better.

Seb could take a break from his issues and move forward. Work was not going well, it was alright. He could start the next day again. Kenny wanted to do the same. But his struggles were always there, like background music, always playing, making it difficult for him to listen to the voice of calm. His struggles simmered inside him and could rise up at any time. It was not just one thing; it was everything. Getting out of bed, putting on clothes, answering a message, and making a decision, each of these was a battle.

Moreover, he could not say, *"Okay, I will not worry about getting out of bed today. I will think about it tomorrow."* Because if he continued to stay in bed, he knew the background music would only get louder, and his life would lose its voice somewhere.

The combination of anxiety and depression that Kenny was going through was a perfect recipe for disaster. It was like a dish that should not be ingested together, yet always seemed to coexist like a buy-one-get-one offer. No one understood why.

There were times when Kenny was jealous of Seb. Seb's life seemed simple and lighter. His problems had beginnings as well as endings. There were solutions and ways to move on or move away. However, Kenny's problems seemed endless, devoid of any true solution. It was obviously not fair to be jealous, but Kenny could not help it.

Kenny knew the fact that his friend's problems were definitely real. However, they seemed to have a path forward, a way to work through them with defined steps or within some timeframe. Seb could talk to his wife, resolve issues in the marriage, and take active steps to improve it. The issues obviously terrified Seb, but at least he knew what needed to be done.

What frustrated Kenny the most was how Seb's problems, though real, seemed to have a clear path forward. Complete with a way to work through those problems with defined steps and timelines. Seb had a roadmap, even if it was difficult to follow. For Kenny, it was a different story. His problems did not come with clear solutions or timelines. They were often unending, or at least seemed that way, unspoken and impossible to explain. How would he tell Seb that he would love to hang out with him, but he could not get out of bed? Seb would ask very relevant questions: *"Are you injured? Is there some physical pain?"*

It was difficult to explain that there was no physical pain. No wound, no broken bone. However, mentally, there was consistent, persistent pain. A pain that was silent, unseen, and in the moment felt unhealable. The wound was not bleeding. Painkillers would not help. However, some weight existed, and it made it difficult for Kenny to get out of bed. And that was it.

The only thing Kenny wanted the most in his life was to experience the simplicity of being able to rise, move through the day, and do something as ordinary as doing dishes without the crushing weight of depression holding him down. It felt like such a small, simple wish. But in his world, it seemed nearly impossible, as if the dishes were just beyond his reach.

30 Suicide bereavement

The death of someone you care about is often painful, but the grief felt by family members, loved ones, and friends can be more complex when the cause of death is suicide. Common grief emotions, such as sadness, yearning, and loneliness, are frequently coupled with additional psychological burdens. Suicide bereavement can cause people to struggle with questions of responsibility, asking themselves, *"Could I have prevented this?"*, making them feel guilty. Heightened trauma reactions, such as nightmares or intrusive images, particularly if the death was violent and unexpected. It can also cause feelings of abandonment, especially in cultures where suicide is still taboo due to the intentional nature of the death. Social discomfort around discussing suicide can lead the bereaved to feel unsupported by family and friends. Others might not be interested in you, but rather interested in the story of the person who committed suicide and want to know every detail about how they did it. On the other hand, conversations with peers who have also lost someone to suicide can enhance feelings of understanding over time.

The psychological impact of suicide bereavement can have severe consequences. Jordan and McIntosh (2011) point out that suicide survivors are at greater risk for depressive disorders, post-traumatic stress, and suicidal ideation themselves. Pitman et al. (2024) argue that, due to this greater risk, support from mental health professionals may be needed for an extended period.

Part of suicide bereavement is that there are three questions which the people left behind always have after a suicide. The first two questions are why the person chose to end their life and what their last words were. Sometimes a suicide note, a voicemail, email or a text might provide some clarity, but at the same time, it can raise more questions. Given the complexity of suicide, there is often not a single explanation for why they committed suicide. The third question is whether he or she suffered. Even knowing that the act itself was not painful and that the person died immediately can give them a form of comfort.

Even though grief is a normal and healthy part of the healing process, it should not be viewed as poor coping. Everyone experiences grief differently. Typically, the intensity of grief fluctuates, with brief periods of relief between emotional episodes. Kübler-Ross (1969) identified five stages of grief. The first stage is denial. It is a coping strategy which acts as a buffer against immediate overwhelming pain and shock. The second stage is anger. People start to ask themselves how this can happen to them. The third stage is bargaining. At this stage, people seek to do everything to escape the situation, using the *'if only'* dialogue. The fourth stage is depression. People realise that their situation is real and begin to mourn. The fifth stage is the acceptance stage. People start to give their grief a place and focus on the future.

As mentioned earlier, grief can be hard to cope with, especially when (professional) help is not available. It is important to know that healing from suicide bereavement is possible, although it might take time and patience. The pain can be magnified if they feel rejected by others. Suicide family and friends (2001) gives some suggestions:

- If you notice signs of depression or suicidal thoughts in yourself or other family members, it is important to seek professional assistance. It is not a sign of weakness to do so.
- Surround yourself with nurturing people, and take time for yourself when you need it.
- Friends and family may seem awkward, uncomfortable, or not know how to help. Speak with them about your needs. Some may not be able to offer the kind of support you need, which is okay.
- Accept that some friends will not be able to give you the kind of emotional support you need. Consider joining a support group in your area or online.
- Be aware that important events, such as birthdays, Christmas, Diwali or Ramadan, will provoke strong feelings.
- Remember that you are allowed to feel positive, happy, and hopeful for the future. How long you grieve is not a measure of how much you loved the person who died.
- Using rituals can help with grieving by marking significant occasions and commemorating the life of the person who has died. These can include lighting a candle, listening to special music, reading poems, or looking at photos.
- Be honest with children and explain suicide in language appropriate to their age.

31 Burnout

Burnout is a serious issue that can significantly impact suicide gatekeepers, those who regularly support people in crisis. It occurs when ongoing stress is left unaddressed, gradually depleting emotional, mental, and physical resources. For gatekeepers, repeated exposure to crisis, despair, and high responsibility can create a constant state of alertness, leaving little chance for recovery. Over time, sustained stress can lead to emotional exhaustion.

Maslach et al. (1997) suggest that burnout has three dimensions. The first dimension is cynicism or depersonalisation. Gatekeepers and caregivers may start to distance themselves and/or develop negative, detached attitudes toward their work. Tasks that once felt meaningful might seem overwhelming or pointless, and motivation can decline. The second dimension is emotional exhaustion. Feelings of emotional numbness, irritability, and reduced empathy may appear not because the people with burnout no longer care, but because their capacity to care has been exhausted. The third dimension is a reduced sense of efficacy, which is a feeling of being unproductive or ineffective. This is particularly a concern if this hits suicide gatekeepers, as they, for example, might not have a supportive conversation or avoid asking direct questions about suicide.

A burnout develops over time. It is important to recognise and acknowledge the signs so that self-care and peer support can help reduce or prevent potential burnout.

32 Moral injury

Suicide prevention gatekeepers have a key role in identifying risk and intervening when a person is in a crisis and vulnerable. When the stakes are high and fast action is expected, they might find themselves unable to provide aid. Those limitations are not necessarily only physical. They may also be exposed to ethical conflicts, traumatic events, and perceived failures in their actions, which can result in moral injury. But what is a moral injury? VanderWeele et al. (2025) define moral injury as: "The distressing psychological, behavioural, social, and sometimes spiritual aftermath of exposure to events that transgress an individual's values and moral values." Being unable to prevent a suicide, following policies perceived as harmful, or witnessing systemic neglect are examples of how a moral injury can develop. Vaknin and Vered Ne'eman-Haviv (2025) propose a (theoretical) model which explains the development of a moral Injury.

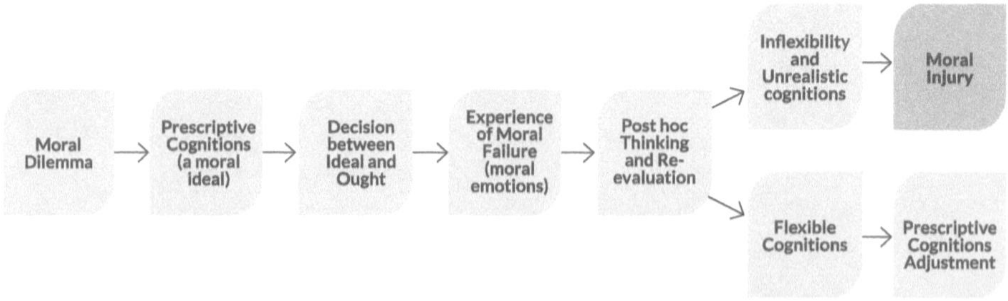

In a suicide gatekeeper context, several morally injurious exposures can happen. Examples are: involving the death of a person despite appropriate intervention, witnessing repeated suffering without adequate resources, system-level constraints, and perceived responsibility. It can also go so far as to feel betrayed by institutions designed to protect life. So this is different from traditional trauma responses, where people respond to actual or potential life-threatening events where they themselves are concerned, which puts them in a fight or flight mode. For suicide prevention gatekeepers, these two domains frequently overlap. Many experience both threat-based trauma symptoms and moral injury simultaneously, resulting in shared outcomes such as depression, anxiety, anger, insomnia, substance misuse, nightmares, and suicidality. Williamson et al. (2020) found that over time, this can erode professional identity and personal meaning. particularly when gatekeepers feel alone or unsupported following a suicide death, persistent guilt, shame, self-condemnation, and hopelessness can cause such psychological pressure that suicide ideation is more likely to be seen as an option by them. Behaviourally, gatekeepers may withdraw from colleagues, disengage emotionally from clients, or increase reliance on substances as a means of coping. From a social perspective, moral injury can contribute to alienation and difficulty maintaining close relationships, as Bryan et al. (2018) note.

It is important to have effective support available for them. The Dutch suicide helpline 113, for example, has a facilitated reflective practice and peer support following suicide-related events. Other measures could include creating and maintaining an organisational culture that acknowledges distress, with leadership accountability and moral dialogue. Jinkerson (2016) highlights that compassion-focused therapy, acceptance-based approaches, restorative practices, and interventions that support meaning-making, self-forgiveness, and values reconnection truly help.

33 Resilience

Being a suicide gatekeeper comes with challenges. At times, they face situations that test a person's ability to cope with difficulties, spirit, and resilience. But what is resilience? McGladrey (2020) defines it as:

"The process and outcome of successfully adapting to difficult or challenging life experiences, especially through mental, emotional, and behavioural flexibility and adjustment to external and internal demands."

Resilience is not a fixed trait but a dynamic process that exists along a continuum from well-resourced to critically injured. Southwick and Charney (2012) note that it is not simply "bouncing back" from a situation or traumatic experience. Being resilient gives people a powerful sense of mission and purpose. Antonovsky (1987) found that this buffers the effects of stress and encourage psychological well-being.

There are four stages in resilience: ready, reacted, injured and critically injured. Gatekeepers in the "ready" stage tend to be spiritually, emotionally, and physically healthy, emotionally available to others, and able to maintain healthy sleep patterns. They have sufficient space in their brain to tolerate the difficult conversations they often have with a person in crisis. Bonanno (2004) points out that this state does not imply the absence of stress, but rather the presence of adequate internal and external resources to meet challenges without becoming overwhelmed.

However, as stress accumulates and/or resources are consumed, those same gatekeepers may shift into a "reacting" stage, exhausting their resilience. They may become more critical of their peers or of the person in crisis, lose interest, lack motivation, or have sleep issues. Life feels "bleh" to them, and they are often easily annoyed. McEwen (2007) notes that these are early warning signs that the coping capacity starts to decline and is being stretched beyond what the person can handle. At this stage, help can prevent additional decline, Hobfoll (2011) describes. This can be accomplished by social support, increased self-awareness and early intervention.

If stress continues unchecked and no help has been sought, resilience can erode further. This may lead to the emotional "injury" stage. Emotional unresponsiveness, avoidance, burnout, exhaustion, and physical symptoms may emerge, along with disengagement and an increased likelihood of mistakes. In the most severe cases, the stage of "critical injury", people may experience hopelessness, anxiety, depression, intrusive thoughts, and a serious sense of loss of control. Feelings of self-blame, relational breakdown, panic, and even thoughts of suicide can arise when psychological and social resources are severely depleted (Joiner, 2005; Shneidman, 1993). Understanding resilience through this continuum highlights an essential truth: resilience is not about persisting endlessly, but about recognising one's position on the spectrum and actively restoring depleted resources. Early recognition, compassion, connection, and organised support are key mechanisms for moving back toward a resourced and sustainable state of wellbeing.

Resourced ⟵⟶ Depleted			
READY	**REACTING**	**INJURED**	**CRITICALLY INJURED**
• Sense of mission • Spiritually & Emotionally healthy • Physically Healthy • Emotionally Available • Healthy sleep • Enjoying • Sense of joy / Vitality • Room for complexity	• Critical of rescuers or patients • Avoiding rescue types • Loss of interest • Distance from others • Short Fuse **Changes:** • Life feels "bleh" • Lack of motivation • Fatigue / weariness • Sleep disturbance	• Sleep Issues • Emotional Numbness • Avoidance • Burnout • Nightmares • Disengaged • Exhausted • Physical Symptoms • "I usta" • Careless mistakes	• Hopelessness • Anxiety • Depression • Intrusive thoughts • Feeling lost or out of control • Thoughts of suicide • Self-blame • Hiding out & Broken relationships • Panic • Suicide

Resilience is about harnessing inner strength, drawing on support systems, and developing coping strategies that support suicide gatekeepers to better deal with crisis situations. So the question is, how can suicide gatekeepers harness themselves? Ginsberg and Jablow (2015) developed the so-called "7 Cs" framework to help build resilience: competence, confidence, connection, character, contribution, coping and control. Competence entails continuous learning and the development of new skills to handle situations effectively. This can be accomplished through training, peer reviews, or other forms of education that push your boundaries and require problem-solving skills. Confidence is about believing in one's own abilities and cultivating a positive self-image. Self-affirmation and the celebration of achievements help increase confidence. Failures should be seen as learning opportunities. Connection is all about building strong ties. Developing these relationships may not only offer emotional support but also expose gatekeepers to diverse perspectives and coping strategies. It will also increase the sense of belonging, empathy and understanding, especially after a tough conversation about suicide. Character is all about values, ethics and integrity. Staying with one's moral compass helps, just as long as the actions and means are aligned with that compass, even when faced with resistance. The contribution concerns the discovery of meaning and purpose. Gatekeepers already serve a purpose in finding a way to stop the person from committing suicide. It is not that they seek applause or want to win awards; it is more about realising that they already make a positive impact on others' lives, which can help renew their strength and motivation. One essential tool for resilience is coping. Learning healthy strategies to manage stress is important as it allows the suicide gatekeeper to deal with difficult situations. Practices such as mindfulness, going to the gym, keeping a journal, or having a hobby all help redirect your mind away from work-related stress. Control focuses on the realisation that the gatekeeper can control their reactions to events. It is about letting go of what cannot be changed and embracing what one can influence.

34 Come back to Earth: A conversation with Vanessa Torres

by Sadiyah Reyal

There is a technique Vanessa Torres discovered for bringing someone back from the edge of panic. You count with them. Fingers on a surface, or against the chest, or pressed into the palm of a hand. One, two, three, four. Something tactile. Something that gives the body a rhythm to hold when the mind has lost its footing entirely. She used it on hundreds of patients over nearly thirty years. She also, during the worst period of her own life, used it on herself.

One, Two, Three, Four.

The paramedic, alone. Counting. Tapping her own chest. Trying to give herself the same anchor she had spent a career giving to others. There is something in it that feels like the whole of what she has to say.

But I want to start somewhere else. I want to start in a hospital corridor in Portland.

* * *

She was working in a trauma bay in Portland when the woman came in. A horse had rolled onto her and caused an open pelvic fracture, the kind of injury that does not leave much room for outcomes other than the worst one. The woman coded. The room filled with the particular controlled chaos of a team doing everything at once and very fast. Vanessa was one of them. And at some point in the middle of all that noise and urgency, she leaned down close to the woman's ear and said: *My name is Vanessa. There are a lot of people in this room. We are doing everything we can.*

The woman was dead when she heard it. No sign of a heartbeat.

Two months later, the same woman stopped Vanessa in the corridor. She was in a wheelchair. She was alive, which was itself a small miracle Vanessa had not expected.

You were the only one who told me your name.

When I first heard this story from Vanessa, I did not know what to do with it. Not because it was difficult to understand, but because it was too clean, too perfectly shaped, the kind of thing that happens in feel-good films precisely because it seems too generous for ordinary life.
Except it happened. In a corridor. To a woman who had been dead.

We have been conditioned, most of us, to be suspicious of warmth that arrives without warning. To look for the architecture behind it, the training, the intention. And yet there was no architecture.

There was no script. She just always told people her name. She did not know exactly why. She just did.

That is the whole of it, really. The rest is context.

* * *

Every other chapter in this book deals with people in crisis or with those who try to reach them. Vanessa Torres is both, but what makes her story worth examining slowly is the sequence. She spent three decades being the one who arrived. The one who knew what to do. She absorbed it all, quietly, professionally, and somewhere in that long accumulation she came to believe, without ever quite saying it, that the absorption had made her immune.

It had not. It had only delayed the bill.

After she retired, a health issue unrelated to her work opened something she had kept sealed for three decades, and all those calls came back. Not in order. Not politely.

Swirling.

She says, and the word is precise: not a flood but a vortex, everything at once. She knew what PTSD was. She had helped hundreds of people through it. And still she told herself: this cannot be what is happening to me.

It was. She went on a watch. Her husband stayed home from work. Her parents came over. She could not be left alone. She found a therapist, started medication, and eventually turned a corner.

And then, in the turning, something unexpected happened to her understanding of everything she had done before. Because going through her own crisis did not diminish what thirty years had built in her. It completed it. Before her breakdown, she used to look at the patients on those calls, the ones who wanted to die, the ones who could not explain the weight of what they were carrying, and wonder why they could not simply snap *out of it.*

Why could they just not feel that way?

The distance between a professional who understands crisis and a human being who has lived inside it, what is it called?

It is not just empathy, though it involves empathy. It is not just experience, though it requires experience. Suffering gave her something she could not have gotten any other way: an authority about human pain that no training program in the world certifies. I believe this.

I believe it because I know something about the way pain accumulates in silence. About how the feelings you do not name do not disappear. They wait. They compound interest in the dark, and the longer you leave them there, the more violently they collect when the door is finally opened. There is a version of understanding that lives only in the body, earned only through having been inside the thing you thought you were studying from a safe distance. It cannot be transferred by lecture or literature. It arrives uninvited, in the night, swirling.

Suffering is not a credential. But it is an accolade. And Vanessa Torres has earned hers in full.

* * *

People, she told me, have a mythology about this job. They imagine it as constant adrenaline, sirens and urgency, lives suspended at the edge of catastrophe. What they do not imagine is the man who could not reach his television remote.

He had suffered a stroke. His caregiver had left for the day. The remote was on the other side of the room, and he was in his chair, and he would be staring at a blank wall until morning. So he called 911. And Vanessa went. And she handed him his remote and stayed for a while, because she could see that the remote was not the point.

She told me this with the warmth of someone recounting a favourite call, not a frustrating one. She loved that man. He was one of her regulars.

This is what gets lost in the abstraction of crisis work: that the range of what counts as a cry for help is enormous and often unglamorous. The elderly who call at ten o'clock at night about a sound in the wall, who are not afraid of a fire but of the silence. The people who call about hangnails and end up talking for forty minutes about something else entirely. A career at the edge of human crisis is also, unavoidably, a career in human loneliness. In the ten thousand ordinary ways, a person can be left without someone to turn to.

The willingness to show up for the small thing, because the small thing is almost never only the small thing, is the same quality that makes you lean down to a woman in cardiac arrest and say your name.

Presence is not calibrated by the severity of the emergency. It is simply presence.

She learned this early. In Fort Worth, at the beginning of her career, she had a mentor twice her age who told her that story time was essential. After every night shift, the crew would drive to a park at six in the morning, open a pack of beer, and talk through everything that had happened that week. They would laugh, mostly. Genuinely, even about the terrible things, especially about the terrible things. She kept a journal in those years that she still has. She eventually turned the calls into books. The people who struggle most in this work, she told me, are those who have nothing outside it. No other life, no other language, nowhere to put what the job gives them to carry. You have to tell it, in whatever form you have. You have to name it, or it names you.

There is a detail she mentioned almost in passing that I have not been able to set down. Not until Vanessa had her own crisis did her mother tell her that at fifteen, she had been deeply depressed. That she had thought she might kill herself. That she had told her father, and he had helped her, and she had never spoken of it again. Decades of silence.

And Vanessa's response was not relief that her mother had survived, nor anger that she had been kept from it. It was a simpler, more unsettling question: why did you never tell me? Because the silence had travelled. The thing unspoken in one generation had no name in the next, and so when it arrived, as it will, it arrived in the dark. This is what the book you are holding is also trying to interrupt. Not the crisis itself, but the inherited silence around it.

* * *

She trained new paramedics for much of her career, and she gave them a mantra she instructed them to return to again and again: this is not your emergency. This is their emergency. You are the finder and the fixer. But this is not happening to you.

It is a necessary instruction. Without some version of it, the work becomes impossible. The pain around you floods the room, and you stop being useful to it. The line is a professional mercy, of sorts.

And yet I received that line differently than I might have expected. Because I am a paramedic in my own life; aren't we all?

Not literally, not the profession, but in the way that matters for this conversation: I am someone who arrives, or at least desperately tries to. Don't we all, for the people we love? Someone for whom other people's emergencies have a way of becoming, very quickly and very completely, my own. The friend in crisis at midnight, the family member coming apart at the seams, the person in the room who is not saying what they mean. I feel the pull of these the way I imagine Vanessa feels the pull of a call: as something that requires me, that I am equipped for, that I cannot in good conscience ignore.

The hard lesson is that absorbing another person's emergency does not resolve it. The person you are trying to help does not become lighter because you have become heavier. They remain exactly as they were. You, meanwhile, are now carrying two loads, and the second one was never yours to carry, and you will feel the strain of it long after the emergency has passed. This is not a failure of love. It is a misunderstanding of what love, in crisis, can actually do.

But I wonder, listening to her, whether any line drawn between a person and thirty years of human suffering actually holds. Whether the compartment you construct for all those calls ever truly stays closed. Her husband, also a paramedic and first responder, kept his sealed for months after the shift that should have broken him: four children dead in a single twenty-four hours, two adults, a mother running down a road with her clothes on fire, a baby still strapped into a car seat, burning.

I'm okay. I'm okay. I'm okay, Vanessa.

He said it the way you say it when the culture around you has made anything else feel like a failure of character. He kept saying it for months. And then one day, he called her from work, and he was whispering.

I don't know what's wrong with me.
This man who ran toward fires. Who stayed functional on scenes that

would hospitalise most people with shock. Who had built, across a long career, the particular interior architecture of someone who does not fall apart. And when the architecture finally gave, he whispered. As though what had broken through deserved to be kept small. As though the pain needed an apology for arriving.

There is a specific cruelty in the culture that produces that whisper. The culture that asks its helpers to be superhuman and then receives any evidence of their humanity as a kind of failure. Vanessa does not say this with anger. But she says it with a clarity that feels hard-won. She would like quarterly mental health check-ins in every department. Consistent messaging. An open-door policy that is not only open on paper.

She is not describing a revolution; she is describing basic care. The fact that it does not yet exist, not reliably, not everywhere, is its own kind of emergency.

This is not your emergency, said to a man whose whole identity was built around being the one who did not fall apart, becomes, at a certain point of accumulated weight, a sentence the body simply refuses to honour. You can draw the line. You cannot always make it hold.

What she has come to understand is that the goal was never imperviousness. The goal was to stay functional long enough to help. The line is a tool, not a truth. And when it breaks, what you need is not shame. What you need is someone who counts with you.

* * *

Her grandmother could read and write very little. She attended school through the third grade, then left to help her mother run a boarding house, and never went back. What she had in place of letters was story. The old Mexican stories, the ones about spirits and omens and La Lechuza, the shapeshifting owl-woman who comes at night to guide souls to the afterlife. She would sit at the kitchen table making tortillas and she would tell them, and Vanessa would listen.

Vanessa has written two novels (Torres, 2022) (Torres, 2025). One is built from those stories: a girl who is a Lechuza by night, who escorts the dead toward wherever they go, who falls in love with one of her passengers and cannot bring herself to release her. A story about the terrible weight of holding on. About what it requires, finally, to open your hands.

There is a lineage in this that I find remarkable. A woman who could not read, sitting at a kitchen table, putting the old stories into her granddaughter's hands. The granddaughter who grew up to spend thirty years in the company of the dying, who eventually wrote those stories into books. A narrator in L.A. who read the audiobook and contacted Vanessa to say it felt as if it were written for me. Story travelling the way Vanessa's grandmother understood story to travel: not through publication channels or literary prizes, but from mouth to ear, from generation to generation, finding the person who most needed to receive it.

This is what the book you are holding is also trying to do. Not to explain suicide from a safe distance, but to carry something forward so

that the person who needs it most finds it, and recognises it, and feels less alone inside what they are carrying.
The grandmother inspired a book she will never read. Vanessa said this simply, without sentimentality, and it is the sentence of someone who has learned to hold the dead without being pulled under by them. She wishes with all her heart that her grandmother could read what she inspired. I asked:
Is that grief? What is grief?

She said:
Grief is gratitude with nowhere left to go, which is perhaps the most durable form of love there is.

* * *

There is something I want to name about what it is like to be in conversation with Vanessa Torres, because I think it is directly relevant to the book's larger argument about what actually reaches people in crisis.

Vanessa creates, without apparent effort, a space in which you feel safe enough to approach the things you would normally keep at a careful distance. Not because she softens them. She does not. She will tell you, with complete equanimity, about a mother running down a road on fire, about a baby in a car seat, about a man who shot himself in the garage minutes after playing a video game with his wife, and she will tell you these things in the same measured tone she uses to describe everything else. She does not protect you from what she has seen. But she is so evidently at peace with the weight of it, so clearly unafraid of the darkness she has spent her career inside, that her presence becomes a kind of permission. You can look at this, she says without saying it. You do not have to look away.

I could have talked with her for hours. I had the particular sense, rare enough to be worth naming, that she would not judge me for my thoughts even if she opposed them. That she has sat with too much real human complexity to be threatened by the ordinary contradictions a person carries. That she is, in the truest sense of the phrase, a safe person. The discomfort she creates is the productive kind: the discomfort of being in the presence of someone so genuinely at ease with difficult things that you begin, almost against your will, to lower your own defences around them.

And this is not incidental to the book's argument. This is the book's argument. The researchers, clinicians, and crisis protocols are not wrong. But what they are describing, at their best, is a reproduction of this: one person whose presence makes another feel that they can speak the unspeakable. Who offers not solutions but ground. Who is so comfortable in the room with whatever you bring into it that your own discomfort begins, almost involuntarily, to ease.

That is not a credential you can earn in a training course. It is built, like Vanessa built it, across decades of choosing to stay.

* * *

One.

She is in a trauma bay in Portland. A woman's heart has stopped. Everyone is doing everything necessary. And Vanessa leans down and says her name.

Two.

She is on a scene. There is a broken child. The other responders are fathers. Vanessa steps forward: I have it. She carries the weight so that the fathers in the room will not carry it home. She is still carrying it now. She will carry it always. You just learn, she says, to think about it in a somewhat healthy way.

Three.

She is alone, months after retiring. The calls are back. She counts. One, two, three, four. Tapping her own chest. Using on herself the only technique she knows works, the one she figured out without a manual, the one she does not know the formal word for and does not need to.

Four.

She is in a conversation with me, telling me about the corridor, and something opens in my chest in the way things open when real life briefly exceeds what you believed real life could offer. Not sentiment. Not performance. Just a person who spent thirty years doing the hardest thing quietly, and survived it, and came out the other side with her name still fully hers.

She built this across thirty years of telling the truth about what she saw. In a park at six in the morning. In a journal she still has. In books born from her grandmother's kitchen table. What she was doing, in all of it, was the same thing she did in that trauma bay: refusing to let the weight go unnamed. Insisting on the human in the room.

The woman in the corridor remembered it. That is what I want to leave you with. Not the technique, not the training, not the accumulated professional wisdom of three decades on the front lines of human crisis, though all of it matters. What the dying woman carried back into her living life was a name said aloud in a room full of noise, by someone who did not have to say it and said it anyway.

My name is Vanessa. There are a lot of people in this room. We are doing everything we can.

One, two, three, four.

Come back to the room.

35 Self-compassion

People in general seem to find it hard, and for some, almost impossible, to treat or speak to themselves in a kind or caring manner. They tend to be harsh on themselves, even when it is unjustified, being their own worst critics. It is easier to self-criticise than to be self-compassionate. Labelling, 'should' statements, and generalising are considered typical forms of self-criticism. For people who are experiencing intense emotional pain, caregivers and suicide gatekeepers helping those people in crisis, self-compassion is often very difficult, and if they do it, it will help them to balance their emotions. But what is self-compassion? Neff (2012) defines it as:

"Being open to and moved by one's own suffering, experiencing feelings of caring and kindness towards oneself, taking an understanding, non-judgemental attitude towards one's inadequacies and failures, and recognising that one's own experience is part of the common human experience."

In short, self-compassion is compassion directed toward oneself. It offers an alternative to self-criticism, shame, and exhaustion for both those who attempt suicide and those who walk alongside them. Self-compassion has four elements: awareness, normalising, kindness and alleviation. All four of these elements should be done to achieve self-compassion. However, they first need to balance their emotions. Gilbert (2009) states that our emotions are governed by three systems. The first system is the threat system, which warns us and protects us against danger, triggering behaviours such as fight, flight, freeze, or fawn. When people are in this mode, they tend to be negative and have a limited tolerance window. The second system is the drive system. This stimulates trying new things and achieving goals. If not addressed, the threat system can easily take over, potentially triggering a downward spiral. The third system is the soothing system. It can be described as a relaxed state in which everything is under control and in harmony, and the drive or threat system is not consuming any emotional space.

Self-compassion can be seen as three interrelated and mutually supportive aspects: self-kindness, common humanity, and mindfulness. Each of these is important for both those in suicidal crisis and those who care for them. For people who have attempted suicide, self-kindness means treating themselves with care and avoiding harsh self-criticism or shame. Self-kindness offers space to support oneself with compassion during difficult moments and to accept oneself unconditionally, rather than punishing oneself. This is different for caregivers and gatekeepers. It is important for them to, without blaming themselves, recognise their own fears, grief, irritations or emotional fatigue.

Common humanity emphasises people's shared struggles, imperfections, and interconnectedness. It fosters belonging and compassion over loneliness and isolation. This interconnectedness is a gift. For caregivers, understanding that they are not alone in helping people with suicidal thoughts is important. Knowing that many colleagues in their field experience doubt, fear, and emotional exhaustion as well can reduce the pressure to execute everything perfectly. People contemplating suicide often feel alone and believe their pain isolates them. Recognising that others also face struggles with hopelessness and failure can reduce shame and build connection.

Mindfulness helps both people in crisis and caregivers acknowledge their suffering honestly, without denial or exaggeration. A definition of mindfulness is a humanistic approach of paying attention, non-judgmental and in the present moment. It is a quality of behaviour often associated with being considerate and a practice often associated with mediation and mindful pauses. It involves an understanding of the mechanisms of psychological distress and the wisdom that leads to freedom from patterns of suffering. For caregivers, mindfulness helps them stay present without becoming overwhelmed or reactive while having a crisis conversation. It helps them notice their own limits, feelings, and signs of exhaustion—things essential for sustainable care. Mindfulness can be beneficial for a person contemplating suicide as it creates space in the mind between the psychache and the urge to escape.

By being gentle with ourselves, recognising our mutual humanity, and staying aware of our feelings, both those in crisis and caregivers can find ways to endure, connect, and grow. When life feels overpowering, self-compassion quietly becomes a powerful act of survival, for ourselves and for those we care about.

36 Self-esteem and self-reflection

A healthy self-esteem facilitates self-reflection. Self-esteem refers to a person's subjective sense of their own worth and value. Low self-esteem may lead a caregiver or gatekeeper to assume excessive responsibility for another person's choices, struggle with guilt or shame, or avoid reflection out of fear of self-criticism. Improving your self-esteem is all about getting from survival to connection. The connection with self is the basis for connection with others. If people feel good about themselves, they experience a sense of safety, which in turn regulates access to higher cognitive functions. During peer self-reflection sessions, psychological safety is equally important.

Psychological safety is defined by Edmondson (1999) as: "A shared belief held by team members that the environment is safe for interpersonal risk-taking, such as speaking up with ideas, questions, concerns, or mistakes without fear of punishment or humiliation."

This kind of safety is necessary, given the crisis intervention itself and the difficult conversations about suicide. Caregivers and gatekeepers occupy a demanding role. They are often required to remain calm in moments of extreme distress, to hold emotional space for another person's pain, and to make careful decisions under pressure. Nobody is perfect. There is always a chance it might not go the way they expected or hoped. Psychological safety stimulates sharing those struggles with peers, even when other professionals are challenged. Edmondson (1999) notes that psychological safety lays the foundation for outcomes that matter: improvement, quality, resilience, and transformation. Feeling safe is equally important for survivors of suicide attempts. Their broken self-esteem needs to be repaired, and that can only be done in a safe environment.

For everyone involved in a suicide matter, suicide survivors, caregivers and gatekeepers, self-reflection groups also need social safety.
Social safety is defined by Slavich (2020) as: "a state in which individuals feel secure, respected, and valued within their social environment, free from threats, violence, intimidation, and inappropriate or transgressive behaviour."

Respect, trust, and a culture of understanding are important in conversations because, without them, people tend to withdraw, leaving them stuck in their current situation.

Self-reflection is a continuous process: it takes place before, during and after conversations about suicide. Schön (1991) describes two ways of reflection. The first way is reflection in action: This occurs in the moment. While engaging with a person in crisis, caregivers continuously and quietly adjust, monitoring tone, noticing emotional shifts, and responding intuitively without interrupting the flow of care. The second way is reflection on action, which happens after the conversations about suicide with the person in distress.

Both reflections help caregivers and gatekeepers to understand how these inner processes influence their actions. The following points are important to ask oneself:

- Do I have the support of someone else? Always ensure someone supports you.
- Am I clear about boundaries? Decide for yourself what you are willing and not willing to discuss.
- Am I caring for my own well-being? Ensure you get enough sleep and do things that give you positive energy. It will help to reduce the likelihood of burnout and emotional overload.
- What made me respond the way I did?
- What worked, and what did not?
- What did I learn about myself and my practice?

These reflections help caregivers and gatekeepers remain grounded and present, rather than reactive or overwhelmed. This ongoing reflective cycle allows gatekeepers and caregivers to grow without being too judgmental about themselves. Understanding your personal strengths and weaknesses helps you learn how to improve your weaknesses. It allows caregivers to plan skill development intentionally, adopt new approaches thoughtfully, and apply learning in ways that fit.

37 A Story: The middle

Jenkins had always found himself navigating through a maze of relationships, both platonic and romantic. His destiny, however, was a relentless force, steering him from one heartbreak to another. Each time he reached out to seek a form of comfort while being in distress, he was met with the familiar refrain: *"Give it some time. Time is the best healer."*

While Jenkins recognised the truth in those words, he could not help but feel diminished by them. Yes, time may dull the sharpness of pain, but it did nothing to soothe the ache of the present moment. The fact that wounds might heal over time did not make them hurt any less now.

Things were even harder for Jenkins because he had been diagnosed with mental health issues. He was on medication, which helped to some extent, but it did not take away the challenges he faced daily. His struggles were not just about relationships; they were part of a much bigger battle within himself.

He often wondered: How does time truly heal? Is it a passive process that requires no effort beyond waiting? He mused that if he ever broke a bone, he could simply wait it out, letting time work its magic, no cast, no care, just patience. Yet, deep down, Jenkins knew that time, without effort or support, felt more like a cruel observer than a gentle healer.

For Jenkins, healing came not from the ticking of the clock but from connection. Whenever conflict arose in his relationships, whether with friends or lovers, he sought refuge in communication; it was not easy, but he believed in voicing his feelings. The trouble was, he learned the hard way that communication was often a rare luxury.

Take his relationship with Daniel, for example. Daniel was a brilliant man, a political speechwriter gifted in the art of persuasion and public dialogue. Jenkins had assumed that his boyfriend's talent for words would naturally extend to their private life. Surely someone so adept at crafting speeches for ministers would know how to navigate the tender terrain of love and vulnerability.

But Jenkins was wrong. Time and time again, his attempts to connect with Daniel were met with defensiveness. Jenkins would say, *"I feel like you are withdrawing from me, Daniel. I feel like you are happier around other people."*

Daniel's response would always be the same: *"It is not like that. I have been busy. How can you expect me to leave work for you? Alternatively, neglect my family just to visit you?"*

To Jenkins, those words did not feel like an explanation; they felt like a dismissal. They seemed to say: *"I have done nothing wrong, so your feelings are invalid. Your hurt does not matter. Please, just move on."*

Jenkins did not expect perfection. He knew he was not the perfect partner either, far from it. He had made his share of mistakes, some of them truly regrettable. But he always tried to communicate. Even leaning into the discomfort of the moment rather than retreat from it. Jenkins did not want excuses; he wanted understanding. Yet, with Daniel, that understanding felt like a distant dream.

For Jenkins, healing would never come from time alone. It was connection, empathy, and effort that soothed the soul. Without them, time was nothing more than a silent witness, watching the fractures grow deeper.

Daniel often said, *"Give it some time. Time is the best healer."* While Jenkins understood the intent behind those words, he could not help but feel frustrated. Time passing, he realised, was not an apology or a resolution. Problems did not disappear simply because days or weeks went by; they just picked up where they left off, often with even more baggage.

When Jenkins and Daniel nearly broke up, Jenkins tried to communicate, hoping they could work through the issues that had brought them to that point. But Daniel dismissed the effort with, *"It is alright. The breakup or the last conversation no longer bothers me. We just need some time."*

Jenkins was not opposed to taking space. He understood that it is sometimes necessary. However, he also believed that if a relationship was to recover truly, it was essential to revisit the unresolved conversations that had caused the pain in the first place. Without that, the underlying hurt remained unaddressed, slowly creating cracks in the relationship's foundation.

Daniel's approach of leaving everything to time and avoiding hard conversations left Jenkins feeling unheard. It seemed like Daniel thought that time alone could fix everything, but to Jenkins, it was not healing anything. Instead, it was letting their connection fade.

Now, whenever Jenkins and Daniel talk, there is a noticeable distance between them. It is a gap that time has not closed but widened. The unresolved tension is still there, maybe even longer than necessary. Because of that, the relationship feels weaker, too. Jenkins has come to understand that time does not heal trauma. Only the sharp edges fade away. And in the process, it can erode the bonds that once held people together. Time is not a healer; it serves as an eraser. It does not mend what is broken; it just blurs the lines until they are harder to see. Healing, Jenkins realised, requires effort, communication, and acknowledgement of the pain. Without those, time simply fades.

38 A Story: Win every battlefield / Kar har maidaan fateh

Payal has a story she finds both amusing and disappointing. She was suffering from severe depression and suicidal thoughts for five long years. Usually, she hid it well. She taught herself to carry her pain quietly, smiling through exhaustion as though pretending were the only way to survive. But there were days when she simply gave up, days when she did not have the energy to hide that something was terribly wrong.

She came from a slightly conservative background where her family loved her deeply and did everything they could for her. They understood mental illness better than most families around them, yet they were not comfortable with the world knowing about Payal's struggles. They saw it as a taboo, a dark secret that needed to be contained. Payal herself had once believed the same. She felt ashamed of what she was going through. She felt like a burden. She did not want anyone to know that she had tried to harm herself many times. She did not want anyone to know about the versions of her that were broken, angry, and hurting.

But with time, therapy, and clarity, she realised something:
What she was experiencing was not a moral failure but just a struggle. A

phase. Something she went through, not something she was. She now speaks about her depression and suicidal thoughts openly whenever someone asks about her past. To her, they are as much a part of her story as failing an athletic meet or getting scolded by a favourite teacher. Her parents are not fully there yet, and that is okay. They are older, and she is willing to walk ahead at her own pace while allowing them to catch up slowly.

Then came 2024.

Payal thought she was doing better. Her family thought the same. But she had a major relapse. She was living alone for work, and one night, in a moment of complete breakdown, she took pills. When she is unwell, her anger becomes uncontrollable, she gets irritable, overwhelmed, and unable to regulate her emotions.

That night, during a phone call, her parents sensed something was terribly wrong. They immediately called her Tayaji's family, who lived nearby, and asked them to check on her. When they reached her place, they found Payal in a devastated state- delirious, panicked, unwilling to talk, wanting to run away, screaming at anyone who tried to come near, throwing things in anger, begging for space. They stayed with her through the chaos and informed her mother.

Her parents arrived the very next day, took her home, and cared for her. It took months of treatment, therapy, and slow healing before she finally became stable again. Payal's mother remained grateful to Taiji for informing her until one day, she received a call from another relative asking,

"Is Payal doing better now?"

Confused, her mother asked what they meant.

The relative replied smugly,
"We all know what your daughter did. She tried to harm herself, probably over some guy. You should get her married quickly. Better that someone else takes responsibility now."

That conversation shattered her mother. She realised that Taiji had told everyone what had happened and perhaps added a few dramatic details of her own. As her mother tried to talk to other relatives about normal topics, she could sense they already knew. They had discussed it. They had judged it. They had judged her.

Payal, meanwhile, was too busy surviving to think about any of this. She was healing, rebuilding, trying to breathe again. By late 2025, she was doing well, better than ever, working, earning, glowing. Her skin looked good, her face looked happy, and except for a few faint memories, she carried no visible trace of her struggles. Then a family wedding arrived.

Payal attended it with her parents, excited after so long. She dressed beautifully, glowing with confidence, genuinely happy to meet everyone again. But the moment she entered the venue, she saw it, the eyes. The look revealed a judgmental, surprised, and calculating demeanour. Eyes that did not expect to see her and seemed to think, "How dare she show her face after what happened?" All the attendants probably wondered what business she had being happy, glowing, alive. To them, she was supposed to remain a shadow, a whispered story, an example, a cautionary tale. They had already constructed a tragic image of her in their heads: a girl trembling in shame, hiding behind her parents, avoiding conversations, a reminder of misfortune.

Shockingly, the most judgmental among them were the highly educated civil servants, doctors, and people in positions of power. People who should have known better. Her extended family, who once joked with her, teased her, and treated her lovingly, became painfully formal. They did not acknowledge her presence. They did not talk to her normally, clearly expecting something else. Maybe her parents would attend the wedding alone, looking defeated and exhausted. Or maybe that Payal, if she came at all, would stand quietly in a corner, guilty, timid, humiliated.

But she did not.

Payal smiled. She talked. She laughed. Her father could not stop smiling, seeing his daughter thriving. Her mother's heart was overflowing with pride. And that was exactly what disappointed the relatives. They did not know what to do with this version of her.

It hit Payal then. People who have seen you at your worst often want to freeze you in that image. They want to remember you as the broken version of yourself, either because it gives them something to gossip about or because it makes them feel better about their own lives. People do not let you move on as easily as you move on from your own past.

The world often freezes you in your lowest moment. They cling to that version of you, not because it is true anymore, but because it is convenient. It makes them feel safe, superior, entertained, or simply comfortable.

Payal handled it with grace. She ate what she wanted, spoke to whomever she liked, enjoyed the celebration, and left with a smile. Her parents were proud. She was proud, too. But later that night, a bittersweet truth settled inside her:

Human beings have a strange habit. We meet someone after years, and the first thing we remember is the worst thing we heard about them. We do not allow people to grow past the version of themselves that suits our narrative.

Payal realised that society is eager to support you in your downfall but hesitant to accept your rise. Healing is personal, but acceptance is communal, and the community often fails. Gossip travels faster than recovery. Judgment lasts longer than empathy. And people rarely update their image of you, even when you have changed, healed, and transformed completely.

People claim they want their loved ones to heal, but they rarely know how to accept that healed version. They forget that the person who went into the darkness is not the same person who came out of it. Helping someone through mental illness does not end with being there during the breakdown. It continues in how we accept their growth, their healing, and their new identity.

Because the person Payal was before during her depression is gone. The person she was during her psychache and suicide ideation is gone too. The person she is now holds pieces of both, but is new, evolved, different. And being a friend, a relative, a loved one means being willing to accept that new version, not holding them hostage to who they were at their worst.

39 The story behind the stories: Scars to your beautiful

For a long time, I, Jasmine Garg, kept asking myself why I had written about these people. What drew me to their stories, their emotions, their quiet struggles? Why would an advocate in India, surrounded by facts and files, find herself writing about something as fragile and invisible as mental health?

Personally, I think I have always known the answer. But it took co-writing this book and living through each chapter to say it aloud finally. The truth is, these people I wrote about were never strangers to me. They were all representing me, just wearing different names, different faces, different voices, because I have been all of them, at one time or another.

I have been the one who needed help the whole time. However, I got something entirely different instead, offered in good faith but never quite enough. Moving between calm and chaos, feeling yellow one day and deep red the next, was also part of me. It was I who relied on medicines to keep steady, and who felt misplaced in every room but still forced herself to belong. I have ideated suicide and thought about suicide and considered ending it all out of exhaustion.

Being the one angry at others for not understanding me, when I myself had no idea what was happening within me, was hard at times. I have been the one who looked fine from the outside but was barely holding it together myself. Moreover, I have been the one learning, again and again, that an illness of the mind does not make you less human. It just makes you human in a different way.

There was no single moment when it started, and no clear one when it got better. Nevertheless, somewhere along the way, I realised something simple: It is okay not to know, and to fall. It is okay to be confused. However, it is also important to get up, because if you do not, you just keep falling deeper. I have learned that healing is not about becoming a new person. It is about learning to love the person you have been and, at times, still are: the scared one, the messy one, the one who kept trying even when it did not show. It is about forgiving yourself for not being "fine."

There were times my family lost hope in me, and times they found it again. There were people I lost along the way and people I found. Furthermore, there was Pascal, who never left, who celebrated every small step as if it were a giant leap, who never made any victory feel small. In moments like those, I started to believe that maybe I was not beyond repair after all.

Not long ago, I was asked to donate platelets for a friend's wife. Before donating, they asked whether I was taking any medication. I said I was taking vitamins, and then I paused, starting an internal dialogue. Should I tell them about the antidepressants? For a moment, my mind wrestled with itself. Scared of their reaction. If it were blood pressure medicine or diabetes tablets, I would not have hesitated, since it is widely accepted. So why could the other medication not be? Why this silence now? And then I said it simply and quietly. Nothing changed. They did not look at me differently. Nor did they ask awkward questions. It was just another medicine, for another part of the body.

Moreover, that moment stayed with me. Because that is how it should be, that is how I want the world to see it. Maybe that in particular is the real reason I drafted these stories. To make people see that mental illness does not always look like what we imagine. It hides behind laughter, work, smiles, and conversations. It can live quietly inside people who seem perfectly fine.

I wrote these stories because I wanted to make it normal to say out loud what so many whisper in fear. I have felt it all. By sharing these stories, I want to help someone, somewhere, feel a little less strange for feeling too much. And maybe, if I am honest, I wrote them to remind myself that I am still here and can make a difference. That I have lived and am still living through all of it. I have had multiple breakdowns and wanted things to stop and rebuild more times than I can count. And somehow, that is what makes me whole. Because in the end, these stories were not about "them." They were all about me. Just told in different voices, in different rooms of my own heart.

40 Conclusion: Bridge over troubled water

The essence of helping loved ones in need is to understand that our responsibility reaches beyond addressing the visible physical symptoms of a mental health disorder. It involves caring for the emotional pain and the hidden struggles endured within, which are often overlooked. All too often, we see people focus more on the physical consequences of mental illnesses than on the disease itself. Support seems to come only when the repercussions become visible to a third party, as if that visibility somehow validates the suffering.

For example, when someone experiences a panic attack, people look immediately after them. In case a person has self-harm wounds, they are promptly dressed. This is different from mental suffering. The invisible pain, the anxiety or the despair being carried is rarely acknowledged. And most of the time, it is not even addressed. It is as if the world only acts when there is something tangible to see that forces their attention. The emotional suffering remains in the background, overlooked and untreated.

Even the check-ins from loved ones often revolve around questions like, “Did you have another panic attack?” or “Did you harm yourself again?" Are these questions essential? Yes, definitely, but they merely skim the surface, addressing the indicators of a much deeper issue. The questions tend to zoom in on the symptoms but overlook the larger picture. They should be centred on what is needed to ease emotional pain and turmoil, such as love, care, and understanding. It is akin to treating a fever, as the body signals an underlying infection. Reducing the fever may bring temporary relief and help the body heal faster, but real recovery requires addressing the main cause.

This explains why the city of Kota in India has adopted measures like banning ceiling fans or mandating fans with springs in hostel rooms. These decisions seek to curb the visible physical outcomes of mental health crises, such as suicides. While these steps may seem sensible, they reflect a broader societal tendency. People still focus on reducing the outward signs of distress. At the same time, they seem to remain indifferent to the emotional despair and helplessness that drive such actions. It is like prescribing painkillers for a fracture without setting the bone, offering surface-level relief while neglecting the more profound injury.

Society appears content to manage what is tangible, what can be seen by the naked eye. Yet, the real healing of minds, hearts, and spirits does not lie in suppressing the visible consequences but in addressing the invisible struggles. Proper support and recovery are possible only when we move beyond the shallow and tend to the core emotional wounds.
The crux of supporting someone with mental illness is to be there in ways that really matter. While physical consequences are often manageable, the root cause, emotional and mental trauma, frequently

goes unaddressed and unhelped. First aid and immediate care for bodily injuries or panic attacks are undeniably essential, but they are only the first step in a much larger responsibility.

Unfortunately, most people stop at this initial stage. They offer help for the visible physical symptoms, but struggle with the more profound, less tangible manifestations of mental illness. To protect themselves, they become more distant. This response is deeply counterintuitive, as it solely reinforces the isolation and pain of those struggling.

Tragically, many people who survive suicide attempts express profound regret not because they lived, but because they were left emotionally abandoned after their physical wounds were treated. They may have been saved from immediate harm, yet the deeper wounds, the loneliness, despair, and unprocessed pain remained ignored. Physical safety is vital, but healing remains incomplete without handling the emotional consequences. To truly help, all of us must go beyond the surface and offer the consistent, caring support that fosters real recovery.

Invisible pain often weighs heavier than visible wounds, and the intangible suffering of the mind demands just as much love and care as physical ailments. Instead of offering surface-level suggestions like "just try not to think" or "stop overthinking," it is more meaningful to actively support your loved one in ways that help them achieve these goals. Active support can take many forms, perhaps accompanying a friend battling depression to the gym, helping them adopt a healthier lifestyle through your presence and encouragement. It could also mean practical gestures, like bringing or ordering food for them instead of simply asking, "Have you eaten?" or saying, "Please eat." These actions prove that you care about the struggling person. It reminds them they are not alone in this battle and their needs are being looked after. Alternatively, maybe it is as simple as reassuring them that you miss them, enjoy their company, or physically showing up to be there for them. These gestures are not just words; they are actions that can practically help ease overthinking and advance emotional healing.

If your approach to helping someone with mental illness focuses solely on addressing the physical manifestations, you may unintentionally be continuing their more profound pain. Being physically safe while feeling emotionally hollow does little good. It can feel not warm-hearted. It is selfish, too. Wanting someone to stay alive solely because of your attachment to them, regardless of how lifeless they may seem inside, prioritises your needs over their well-being. Proper support is not about keeping someone tethered to life at any cost; it is about helping them find reasons to live and feel whole, truly.

It is important not to limit your presence when your friend explicitly needs you. Of course, being there during emergencies is essential, but genuine support goes beyond those immediate needs. Make plans that go beyond their difficulties, plans that bring joy and build relationships. This simple effort can make struggling people feel really appreciated and needed. It reminds them that they matter, not just because of their pain but because of who they are. These times of inclusion can prevent the experiences of isolation that often fuel suicidal ideations. Please think of how you might visit a friend in the hospital, engaging them in conversations or games to make their stay lighter and more bearable.

Your friends battling mental illnesses need the same kind of effort, a touch of normality, some laughter, and help not just in managing the visible consequences of their condition but in actually fighting the illness within their minds.

Equally important is learning to listen and accept what someone shares about their feelings. If someone opens up to you about their mental state, do not dismiss or invalidate their experience. After all, you would not tell someone with asthma, "There is so much air around you, why can't you just breathe?" In the same way, stop telling someone struggling with mental illness, "There is so much good in your life, why can't you just be happy?" Though often said with good intentions, such words merely deepen the sense of misunderstanding, guilt and isolation. Instead, pay attention to empathy. Accept their emotions without critique or comparison, and let them know they are listened to and supported.

Do not impose a timeline on your friend and expect them to recover from their mental illness by a fixed date you have decided for them. Even physical illnesses can become complicated and take far longer than anticipated to heal, and the brain is still a mystery in many ways, even to doctors and is no exception. Assigning a deadline for someone's mental recovery does not help; instead, it burdens them with guilt if they cannot achieve "optimum mental health" within the time you have prescribed. Healing does not follow a schedule, and it is key to treat it with patience and tolerance.

Equally important is being patient with relapses, a natural part of recovery. Just as a muscle injury might ache again in colder weather, mental illnesses can resurface when triggered by certain events, seasons, or anniversaries of past trauma. The brain, in its altered and chemically injured state, sometimes carries lingering side effects, and these flare-ups are not within anyone's control. Do not blame your loved one for slipping back into their illness or developing a new one. Mental health difficulties often compound; it is like a harsh "buy one, get more" deal. Trust me, they are already having a hard enough time accepting that they are falling back into the depression or anxiety disorder they fought so bravely to overcome. They do not want to relive it any more than you want to see them go through it again.

Your role as a support system is not to fix deadlines or display frustration amid setbacks. It is to stand beside them, unwavering, as they navigate the unstable and often exhausting recovery path. Be patient when they do not seem to be improving despite your support and efforts. Mental illnesses are not easy to navigate, and their journey tends to be far from linear. It can sometimes seem overwhelming, and the struggle may seem never-ending. Mental illnesses can be ugly in their intensity, but one's patience and firm presence will make a difference, even when nothing changes.

Stop asking your loved one to explain the reason behind their illness because, more often than not, there is no clear answer. While there may be triggers, they are rarely the root cause. Some mental illnesses are deeply ingrained, even familial. Those who are struggling with these illnesses are often trying to figure out *why* this is happening to them. It only deepens their sense of confusion and hopelessness when they cannot answer that question. It is difficult to pinpoint a cause; sometimes, triggers remain unidentified for a long time. Even when they are, they often seem scattered and too complex to explain or understand fully.

Do not try to take on the role of their therapist. That is not your responsibility. Doing so will only tire you out; eventually, you may withdraw and feel helpless. Remember, your role is to support them, not to heal them. You can accompany them to appointments with professionals, help them find the right ones, and check in on whether their current treatment is working, but beyond that, do not try to be their psychiatrist or therapist. You do not need to advise them on how to feel better; your presence is enough. The most important thing you can do is be there for them, understanding that your role is not to diagnose or solve. Try to understand their triggers, which they may have learned to recognise in therapy, but resist the urge to identify them independently. Misdiagnosis is far more harmful than not knowing at all. Just as you would not diagnose yourself or a friend with cancer without undergoing proper tests, it is advised not to attempt to diagnose mental health disorders in yourself or your loved ones. Mental health professionals, such as psychologists and psychiatrists, are better equipped to assess and provide accurate diagnoses. Google might offer a list of symptoms, but it is important to remember that it treats everyone equally, while a specialist can provide a tailored, thoughtful diagnosis.

People often label other people. Terms like "depression" or "OCD" are frequently used out of context. It is important to remind ourselves that people are not clinically depressed until a doctor officially confirms it, and one does not have OCD unless a professional diagnoses it. If you notice symptoms consistent with these conditions, seek a doctor's opinion for an official diagnosis. Chances are, you may not be clinically depressed; you might just be experiencing sadness. Similarly, you may not have OCD; you could be someone who values hygiene and order. It is no different from discovering a lump in your throat; you would not immediately assume it is cancer. You would visit a doctor, who might diagnose you with tonsillitis instead of a cancerous tumour.

Understand that mental illness does not always need a reason, just as sometimes you wake up with unexplained pain in random parts of your body or some days you may feel unproductive because depression has taken hold. On other days, the brain may manage to function despite the illness. Similarly, there is no apparent reason why your eyes look the way they do or why your height is what it is. These are purely genetic and formed by a range of factors. The same goes for the brain and mental illness. Sometimes, there is no specific cause for the illness other than genetics, or other factors may come into play.

Trying to be there for your loved ones is helpful and much appreciated, especially during their most challenging moments. It is true that a person's patience will be tested, but remember, it is a shared responsibility, and one must be patient with them. Think about how you would rush to be with a friend who had been in a car accident. If you could, you would drop everything to be by their side. The same principle applies when someone you care about is experiencing severe panic attacks or other mental health crises. Do not hesitate to offer your support as you would for any physical emergency.

Do not overpromise because setting unrealistic expectations can be harmful. When you fail to deliver on those promises, it breaks your loved one's belief in themselves. You cannot promise to heal them. Healing is a journey they must walk. What you can offer is your constant support. Offering false hope and breaking it is far more painful than never offering hope.

It is normal to feel anxious when someone you love is going through a tough time. That anxiety is as natural as the worry you would feel for a loved one in the hospital after an accident or the pit in your stomach when someone close to you is battling a chronic illness. In those cases, you would not think of leaving them because you understand their condition is not within their control.

The same understanding must apply to loved ones with mental illnesses. Do not abandon them because they seem unable to get better or because they relapse. Their mental health, like any other illness, is not something they can control. Walking away from them because your anxiety feels overpowering does not just leave them alone; it sends a message that they are unworthy of love and pushes them closer to the edge.

Leaving them might give you a convenient way to say later, "I wish I knew" or "I could have helped," without needing to try anymore, but that serves no real purpose. If you call someone a loved one, the least you can do is ensure they never feel guilty for how their brain is wired.

Even if you cannot "fix" things, your presence, patience, and refusal to give up can mean the difference between despair and hope for them. Most people living with mental illness are desperately holding on to any trace of hope. A minor act of patience, a kind word, or simply being present can make a difference. Your support, no matter how seemingly small, can ease their pain and remind them that they are not alone.

Never abandon your loved one when they express a need for more love. Walking away because you are unable to provide what they need does the opposite of what they are desperately seeking. While creating boundaries is essential, so is finding a central ground and a space where your desires and theirs can coexist.

It is about fixing communication problems, not resorting to extremes like walking away, which can leave your loved one feeling abandoned. Relationships depend on effort and patience, showing that you are willing to try even in times of change. This list of what to do and what not to do is just a starting point. Every person's journey with mental health is unique, and what works for one could not be effective for another. What really matters is being there for your loved one in a way they need, not just what you think might help. Listen to them, let their voice guide you, and do not hesitate to seek advice from their mental health professional. They can help you understand how best to care for them and offer the support they need. Seeking help is never a sign of weakness; it shows strength, courage and a choice to take a different path than the road to commit suicide.

Last but not least, be proactive, compassionate, and patient. With proper understanding and a readiness to learn, supporting a loved one through their struggles does not have to feel overwhelming. It can become a path of strong connection and growth for both of you. Remember, your love and presence can be the light they need in their darkest moments. Sometimes, just knowing you are there can mean everything. Suicide remains one of the most pressing public health issues globally. It causes immense human suffering and a heavy social impact. Despite all the increased awareness and efforts to improve mental health care, suicide continues to affect people of all ages and backgrounds, with exceptionally high rates among younger people, Generation Z and Alpha and in resource-limited contexts.

41 Worldwide suicide statistics

Global suicide burden

Every year, over 720,000 people worldwide die by suicide, making it a leading preventable cause of death (WHO, 2023). Suicide is a complex phenomenon influenced by social, cultural, biological, psychological, and environmental factors that impact individuals throughout their lives. Its causes are multifaceted and seldom linked to a single reason, including mental health issues, trauma, social isolation, economic hardship, and limited access to care, among others (WHO, 2023).

The impact of suicide on younger populations is particularly concerning. It ranks as the third leading cause of death among those aged 15–29, underscoring its significant effect on adolescents and young adults during critical developmental stages (WHO, 2023). For each suicide death, many more are non-fatal attempts, with a history of prior attempts being among the strongest individual risk factors for future suicide (Turecki et al., 2019). These attempts often result in severe injuries, long-term disabilities, and increased psychological stress.

Suicide in low- and middle-income countries

Suicide, despite garnering global attention, poses a particularly heavy burden on low- and middle-income countries. Around 73% of suicides worldwide happen in these nations, highlighting various vulnerabilities such as poor access to mental health care, economic instability, and stigma around seeking help (WHO, 2023). Nonetheless, only a few countries have established national suicide prevention strategies—currently, only 38 countries have such plans—revealing substantial gaps in global policy and prevention initiatives (WHO, 2023).

Suicide statistics in the Netherlands

The Netherlands, like many high-income countries, continues to face suicide as a significant cause of death. The Commission on Current Dutch Suicide Registration reports 1,849 suicides in 2024, averaging about five per day (CBS, 2025). When considering population size and age distribution, the suicide rate has remained steady in recent years, around 10.3 to 10.9 per 100,000 people (CBS, 2025). However, the impact on youth is notable: suicide is now a leading cause of death among those under 30, aligning with global trends of increased vulnerability among young people (CBS, 2025; 113 Zelfmoordpreventie).

Data from 113 Zelfmoordpreventie show that suicide has been a persistent public health concern in the Netherlands, with about 1,800 deaths each year and a higher impact on men aged 40–70 (113 Zelfmoordpreventie). Historical data indicate that for every suicide, there are roughly 25 attempts, highlighting a much larger group of individuals engaging in serious suicidal behaviour than the official death figures suggest (113 factsheet estimates, 2021).

These statistics also point to broader societal impacts: each suicide affects many others, including family, friends, and communities, with nearly 250,000 individuals in the Netherlands exposed to suicide-related loss each year, highlighting the extensive ripple effects beyond the individual (113 statsheet, 2021).

Suicide statistics in India

India, as the world's second-most populous country, represents a substantial proportion of the global suicide burden. According to government data, approximately 171,000 people died by suicide in India in 2022, with the national suicide rate rising to about 12.4 per 100,000 population, one of the highest recorded in the country's history (National Crime Records Bureau via WHO country profile; WHO, 2025). These figures mean that India accounts for a large share of global suicide deaths in absolute terms, with young people and daily wage earners among the most affected groups (WHO, 2025). National data also highlight significant geographic and demographic patterns. For example, urban centres such as Delhi, Bengaluru, and Mumbai report high numbers of suicide deaths, and men outnumber women in suicide cases by nearly three to one in some major cities (National Crime Records Bureau reports). Additionally, tens of thousands of individuals in the agricultural sector died by suicide in 2023 alone, illustrating the widespread impact across diverse socioeconomic groups (NCRB cited; WHO, 2025).

Suicide statistics in the United States

In the United States, suicide is a major cause of preventable death and a public health concern. According to data from the U.S. Centers for Disease Control and Prevention (CDC), there were nearly 49,500 recorded suicide deaths in 2022, with national suicide rates among the highest in decades, at approximately 14.3 per 100,000 population (WHO and national CDC data, 2025). Suicide rates have risen significantly over time, increasing by roughly 35% between 2000 and 2020, before a slight decline in recent years (WHO, 2025).

While the overall rate varies across states and demographic groups, trends indicate persistent risk among middle-aged adults and elevated rates among males compared with females. The U.S. suicide burden also reflects broader issues, including access to lethal means, mental health care disparities, and social determinants of health.

Suicide statistics in Japan

In 2024, Japan saw around 20,268 people lose their lives to suicide according to Nippon.com (2025), which is the second-lowest number since records started in 1978 and shows a positive downward trend from previous years. This results in a suicide rate of about 16.3 per 100,000 people, giving hope that efforts to address this issue are making a difference after the ups and downs during and after the COVID-19 pandemic. However, some worrying patterns remain. Suicide among schoolchildren and students increased, with about 1,072 deaths among those aged 15–29 in 2024, highlighting that young people are still at risk. Interestingly, for the first time in decades, more girls than boys in this age group took their own lives, with 288 girls compared to 239 boys. Japan also shows gender differences in these statistics. Men have traditionally accounted for about 70% of all suicide deaths. However, recent trends indicate that the risk is present across both genders and seems to be rising, particularly among young women.

Despite the significant impact of suicide worldwide and nationally, prevention efforts are still disjointed. Many nations have not yet made suicide prevention a priority in their health policies. The slow uptake of comprehensive, evidence-based strategies highlights issues such as political will, resource distribution, and stigma. In the Netherlands, recent laws seek to enhance structural support for suicide prevention at the municipal level, but full implementation is still underway, revealing a gap between policy intentions and local actions.

42 List of suicide hotlines per country

Important note

In some countries, especially where dedicated suicide hotlines are limited, emergency services, hospital emergency departments, or government mental health lines may be the primary crisis response. This list is non-exhaustive.

International / Global

- Find a Helpline (IASP) - https://findahelpline.com
  Global directory covering most countries
- Befrienders Worldwide - https://www.befrienders.org
  International suicide prevention and helpline network

Australia

- Lifeline – 13 11 14 https://www.lifeline.org.au
- Beyond Blue – 1300 22 4636 https://www.beyondblue.org.au

Brazil

- Centro de Valorização da Vida (CVV) – 188 https://www.cvv.org.br

Canada

- Talk Suicide Canada – 1-833-456-4566 https://talksuicide.ca
- Crisis Services Canada – https://www.crisisservicescanada.ca

China (Mainland)

- Beijing Suicide Research and Prevention Centre Hotline – +86-10-8295-1332
- Lifeline China – 400 821 1215 https://www.lifelinechina.org (English and Mandarin support in some regions)

France

- Suicide Prevention Number (Numéro national prévention du suicide) – 3114 https://3114.fr

Germany

- Telefonseelsorge – 0800 1110111 or 0800 1110222
- https://www.telefonseelsorge.de

India

- AASRA – +91-22-27546669 https://www.aasra.info
- Sneha Foundation – +91-44-24640050 https://www.snehaindia.org
- Tele Manas +1800-89-14416 or 14416 https://telemanas.mohfw.gov.in/home

Ireland

- Samaritans Ireland – 116 123 https://www.samaritans.org/ireland

Japan

- Yorisoi Hotline – 0120-279-338 https://yorisoi-chat.jp
- TELL Lifeline – 03-5774-0992 https://telljp.com

Netherlands

- 113 Suicide Prevention – 113 or 0800-0113 https://www.113.nl

New Zealand

- 1737 – Need to Talk? – Call or text 1737 https://1737.org.nz

- Lifeline NZ – 0800 543 354 | https://www.lifeline.org.nz

Singapore

- Samaritans of Singapore (SOS) – 1767 https://www.sos.org.sg

South Africa

- South African Depression and Anxiety Group (SADAG) – 0800 567 567 https://www.sadag.org

South Korea

- Suicide Hotline (Ministry of Health and Welfare) 1393 https://www.1393.go.kr

Spain

- Teléfono de la Esperanza – 717003717 https://www.telefonodelaesperanza.org
- Cruz Roja – Línea 024 – 024 https://www.cruzroja.es

Sri Lanka

- Sumithrayo – +94-11-2696666 https://sumithrayo.org
- CCCline (National) – 1333

Taiwan

- Taiwan Suicide Prevention Hotline – 1925 (Life Line) https://www.1925.org.tw
- Teacher Chang Foundation Lifeline – 1980 https://www.1980.org.tw

United Arab Emirates (UAE)

- Mental Support Line (Abu Dhabi Estijaba) – 800-1717 https://www.estijaba.gov.ae (Mental health and crisis support; emergency-focused system)

- National Suicide and Crisis Support (via Estijaba / MOHAP) – 998 (Emergency)

United Kingdom

- Samaritans – 116 123 https://www.samaritans.org
- NHS Urgent Mental Health Helplines – https://www.nhs.uk

United States

- 988 Suicide and Crisis Lifeline – Call or text 988 https://988lifeline.org
- Crisis Text Line – Text HOME to 741741 https://www.crisistextline.org

43 References

113 Zelfmoordpreventie. (2021). Factsheet – Suicide Facts and Figures [PDF]. Retrieved from https://www.113.nl/sites/default/files/113/2020%20middelen/Factsheet-suicide%20facts%20and%20figures.pdf 113 Zelfmoordpreventie

Adam, K. S., Sheldon-Keller, A. E., & West, M. (1996). Attachment organisation and history of suicidal behaviour in clinical adolescents. *Journal of Consulting and Clinical Psychology, 64* (2), 264–272.

Adinkrah, M. (2016). Anti-suicide laws in nine African countries: Criminalization, prosecution and penalization. African Journal of Criminology and Justice Studies, 9, 279–292. https://www.wathi.org/anti-suicide-laws-in-nine-african-countries-criminalization-prosecution-and-penalization/

Agyapong, B., Shalaby, R., Eboreime, E., Kisely, S., Bhatt, M., & Agyapong, V. I. O. (2022). Centering decriminalization of suicide in low- and middle-income countries on effective suicide prevention strategies. Frontiers in Psychiatry, 13, 1034206. https://pmc.ncbi.nlm.nih.gov/articles/PMC9712720/

American Psychiatric Association. (2022). *Diagnostic and statistical manual of mental disorders* (5th ed., text rev.; DSM-5-TR). APA Publishing.

Aquinas, T. (1981). Summa Theologica (Fathers of the English Dominican Province, Trans.). Christian Classics. (Original work published 1265–1274)

Arnsten, A. F. T. (2009). Stress signalling pathways that impair prefrontal cortex structure and function. *Nature Reviews Neuroscience*, 10(6), 410–422. https://doi.org/10.1038/nrn2648

Augustine, A. (2003). The City of God (H. Bettenson, Trans.). Penguin Classics. (Original work published 426 CE).

Baldwin, S. A., Wampold, B. E., & Imel, Z. E. (2007). Untangling the alliance–outcome correlation: Exploring the relative importance of therapist and patient variability in the alliance. *Journal of Consulting and Clinical Psychology*, 75(6), 842–852.

Batson, C. D. (2009). *These things called empathy: Eight related but distinct phenomena*. In J. Decety and W. Ickes (Eds.), The social neuroscience of empathy (pp. 3–15). MIT Press.

Baumeister, R. F., & Leary, M. R. (1995). The need to belong: Desire for interpersonal attachments as a fundamental human motivation. *Psychological Bulletin*, 117(3), 497–529.

Beauchamp, T. L., & Childress, J. F. (2019). *Principles of Biomedical Ethics* (8th ed.). Oxford University Press.

Beck, A. T., Rush, A. J., Shaw, B. F., & Emery, G. (1979). *Cognitive Therapy of Depression.* Guilford Press.

Beck, A. T. (1967). *Depression: Clinical, Experimental, and Theoretical Aspects.* Harper and Row.

Borkovec TD, Robinson E, Pruzinsky T, & DePree JA (1983). Preliminary exploration of worry: Some characteristics and processes. Behaviour Research and Therapy, 21(1), 9–16. 10.1016/0005-7967(83)90121-3

Bowlby, J. (1969). *Attachment and loss: Vol. 1. Attachment.* Basic Books.

Bowlby, J. (1988). *A Secure Base: Parent-Child Attachment and Healthy Human Development.* Basic Books.

Bremner, J. D. (2006). *Traumatic stress: Effects on the brain.* Dialogues in Clinical Neuroscience, 8(4), 445–461.

Bonanno, G. A. (2004). *Loss, Trauma, and Human Resilience.* American Psychologist.

Bremner, J. D. (2006). *Traumatic stress: Effects on the brain.* Dialogues in Clinical Neuroscience, 8(4), 445–461.

Brewin, C. R., Andrews, B., & Valentine, J. D. (2010). Meta-analysis of risk factors for posttraumatic stress disorder in trauma-exposed adults. *Journal of Consulting and Clinical Psychology*, 68(5), 748–766.

Briggs, K. (2015). *Guardian of the Golden Gate: Protecting the line between hope and despair.* New York, NY: HarperCollins.

Brown, B. (2021). *Atlas of the heart: mapping meaningful connection and the language of human experience.* First edition. Random House.

Brown, G. K., & Stanley, B. (2008). Safety planning intervention: A brief intervention to mitigate suicide risk. *Cognitive and Behavioural Practice, 15*(2), 256–264. https://doi.org/10.1016/j.cbpra.2007.01.001

Brown, T. E. (2013). *A new understanding of ADHD in children and adults.* Routledge.

Brownell, J. (2012). *Listening: Attitudes, principles, and skills* (5th ed.). Boston, MA: Pearson

Bryan, C. J., Mintz, J., Clemans, T. A., Leeson, B., Burch, T. S., Williams, S. R., & Rudd, M. D. (2017). Effect of crisis response planning vs contracts for safety on suicide risk in U.S. Army Soldiers: A randomised clinical trial. Journal of Affective Disorders, 212, 264–272.

Bryan, C. J., Bryan, A. O., Roberge, E., Leifker, F. R., & Rozek, D. C. (2018). Moral injury, posttraumatic stress disorder, and suicidal behaviour among military personnel. *Psychological Trauma: Theory, Research, Practice, and Policy, 10*(1), 36–45.

Burleson, B. R. (2010). The nature of interpersonal communication: A message-centred approach. In C. R. Berger et al. (Eds.), Handbook of communication science (pp. 145–163). Sage.

Cassidy, S., Bradley, L., Shaw, R., & Baron-Cohen, S. (2018). Risk markers for suicidality in autistic adults. *Molecular Autism, 9*(42), 1–14.

Centraal Bureau voor de Statistiek (2025) 1 *849 Zelfdodingen in 2024, Centraal Bureau voor de Statistiek*. Available at: https://

www.cbs.nl/nl-nl/nieuws/2025/21/1-849-zelfdodingen-in-2024 (Accessed: 02 January 2026).

Cerel, J., Jordan, J. R., & Duberstein, P. R. (2008). The impact of suicide on the family. Crisis, 29(1), 38–44. https://doi.org/10.1027/0227-5910.29.1.38

Clark, H. H. (1996). *Using language.* Cambridge University Press.

Corey, G., Corey, M. S., & Callanan, P. (2015). *Issues and Ethics in the Helping Professions* (9th ed.). Cengage Learning.

Craske, M. G., Stein, M. B., Eley, T. C., Milad, M. R., Holmes, A., Rapee, R. M., & Wittchen, H. U. (2017). Anxiety disorders. *Nature Reviews Disease Primers, 3*, 17024. https://doi.org/10.1038/nrdp.2017.24

Dazzi, T., Gribble, R., Wessely, S., & Fear, N. T. (2014). Does asking about suicide and related behaviours induce suicidal ideation? *Psychological Medicine, 44*(16), 3361–3363.

Denboba, D., U.S. Department of Health and Human Services, Health Services and Resources Administration (1993). *MCHB/DSCSHCN Guidance for Competitive Applications, Maternal and Child Health Improvement Projects for Children with Special Health Care Needs.*

Earley, P. C., & Mosakowski, E. (2004). Toward Culture Intelligence: Turning Cultural Differences into a Workplace Advantage. Academy of Management Executive, 18, 151-157

Edmondson, A. (1999). Psychological safety and learning behaviour in work teams. Administrative Science Quarterly, 44(2), 350–383. https://doi.org/10.2307/2666999

Ehlers, A., & Clark, D. M. (2000). A cognitive model of posttraumatic stress disorder. *Behaviour Research and Therapy,* 38(4), 319–345.

Enright, R. D., Freedman, S., & Rique, J. (1998). The psychology of interpersonal forgiveness. In R. D. Enright & J. North (Eds.), Exploring forgiveness (pp. 46–62). University of Wisconsin Press.

Everly, G. S., & Mitchell, J. T. (2008). *The Critical Incident Stress Management (CISM) Approach*. Chevron Publishing.

Felitti, V. J., Anda, R. F., Nordenberg, D., et al. (1998). Relationship of childhood abuse and household dysfunction to many of the leading causes of death in adults. *American Journal of Preventive Medicine, 14*(4), 245–258.

Figley, C. R. (2002). *Compassion Fatigue: Psychotherapists' Chronic Lack of Self-Care*. Brunner-Routledge.

Frei, F. & Morriss, A. (2020). Unleashed: The Unapologetic Leader's Guide to Empowering Everyone Around You. Boston, MA: Harvard Business Review Press

Gilbert, P. (2009). Evolved minds and compassion-focused imagery in depression. In L. Stopa (Ed.), *Imagery and the threatened self: Perspectives on mental imagery and the self in cognitive therapy* (pp. 206–231). Routledge/Taylor & Francis Group.

Goffman, E. (1981). *Forms of talk*—University of Pennsylvania Press.

Goleman, D. (1995). *Emotional intelligence.* Bantam Books.

Gould, M. S., Marrocco, F. A., Kleinman, M., et al. (2005). Evaluating the iatrogenic risk of youth suicide screening programs. JAMA, 293(13), 1635–1643.

Gould, M. S., et al. (2003). *The influence of media on suicide. In Suicide and Life-Threatening Behaviour.*

Gunther, M., Maldonado, J. R., & Dickerman, A. L. (2024). Words matter: Why distinguishing medical aid in dying from suicide should matter to a consultation-liaison psychiatrist. Journal of the Academy of Consultation-Liaison Psychiatry, 65(6), 527–536. https://www.sciencedirect.com/science/article/abs/pii/S2667296024000466

Harris, M. & Fallot, R. D. (2001). *Using Trauma Theory to Design Service Systems.* Jossey-Bass.

Harvard T. H. Chan School of Public Health. (2023). *Means matter: Recommendations for clinicians.* Harvard University.

Hawton, K., & Williams, K. (2001). The Papageno effect and audience influences on suicidal behaviour. *British Journal of Psychiatry, 178,* 201–205.

Helton, W. S., & Russell, P. N. (2017). Rest Is Still Best: The Role of the Qualitative and Quantitative Load of Interruptions on Vigilance: The Role of the Qualitative and Quantitative Load of Interruptions on Vigilance. *Human Factors: The Journal of the Human Factors and Ergonomics Society, 59*(1), 91–100. https://doi.org/10.1177/0018720816683509 (Original work published 2017)

Herman, J. L. (1992). *Trauma and recovery.* Basic Books.

Hill, C. E., Thompson, B. J., & Ladany, N. (2003). Therapists' use of silence in therapy: A survey. *Journal of Clinical Psychology*, 59(4), 513–524.

Hirvikoski, T., et al. (2020). Premature mortality in autism spectrum disorder. *British Journal of Psychiatry, 208*(3), 232–238.

Hobfoll, S. E. (2011). *Conservation of Resources Theory: Its Implication for Stress, Health, and Resilience.* Oxford University Press.

Holt-Lunstad, J., Smith, T. B., Baker, M., Harris, T., & Stephenson, D. (2015). Loneliness and social isolation as risk factors for mortality. *Perspectives on Psychological Science, 10*(2), 227–237. https://doi.org/10.1177/1745691614568352

Hom, M. A., Stanley, I. H., & Joiner, T. E. (2017). Evaluating factors and interventions that influence help-seeking for suicidal ideation. *Clinical Psychology Review, 51*, 1–13.

Janis, I. L., & Mann, L. (1977). Decision making: A psychological analysis of conflict, choice, and commitment. New York, NY, US: Free Press

Janoff-Bulman, R. (1992). *Shattered assumptions: Towards a new psychology of trauma.* Free Press.

Jinkerson, J. D. (2016). Defining and assessing moral injury: A syndrome perspective. *Traumatology, 22*(2), 122–130.

Jobes, D. A. (2016). *Managing suicidal risk: A collaborative approach* (2nd ed.). Guilford Press.

Joiner, T. (2005). *Why People Die by Suicide.* Harvard University Press.

Joiner, T. E., Van Orden, K. A., Witte, T. K., & Rudd, M. D. (2009). The interpersonal-psychological theory of suicidal behaviour. *Psychological Review, 117*(2), 575–600.

Joker. Directed by Todd Phillips, starring Joaquin Phoenix and Robert De Niro, Warner Bros. Pictures, 2019.

Jordan, J. R., & McIntosh, J. L. (2011). Grief after suicide: Understanding the consequences and caring for the survivors. Routledge.

Jourard, S. M. (1971). *Self-disclosure: An experimental analysis of the transparent self.* Wiley-Interscience.

Journal of the American Academy of Psychiatry and the Law. (2024). Legal implications of psychiatric assessment for medical aid in dying. https://jaapl.org/content/early/2024/07/26/JAAPL.240042-24

Kabigting, B. et al. (2022). *Avoiding mindlessness with cultural mindfulness, GLOBIS Insights.* Available at: https://globisinsights.com/purpose/dei/cultural-mindfulness/ (Accessed: 02 January 2026).

Katz, R. R., Ogilvie, S., Shaw, J., & Woodhead, L. (2021). *Gen Z, explained: The art of living in a Digital age*—the University of Chicago Press.

Kerns, C. M., et al. (2015). Emotion regulation in autism spectrum disorder. *Journal of Autism and Developmental Disorders*, 45(11), 3400–3413.

Kleiman, E. M., & Liu, R. T. (2013). Social support as a protective factor in suicide: Findings from two nationally representative samples. *Journal of Affective Disorders, 150*(2), 540–545. https://doi.org/10.1016/j.jad.2013.01.033

Kosfeld, M., Heinrichs, M., Zak, P. J., Fischbacher, U., & Fehr, E. (2005). Oxytocin increases trust in humans. *Nature, 435*(7042), 673–676. https://doi.org/10.1038/nature03701

Kurien, R., Paila, A. R., & Nagendra, A. (2014). Application of Paralysis analysis syndrome in customer decision making. Procedia Economics and Finance, 11, 323–334. https://doi.org/10.1016/s2212-5671(14)00200-7

Lester D, McSwain S, Gunn JF 3rd. (2013) Suicide and the Internet: the case of Amanda Todd. International Journal of Emergency Mental Health. ;15(3):179–180. PMID: 24558746.

Lew, B., Lester, D., Mustapha, F. I., Yip, P., Chen, Y.-Y., Panirselvam, R. R., Hassan, A. S., In, S., Chan, L. F., Ibrahim, N., Chan, C. M. H., & Siau, C. S., Mishara, B. L., & Weisstub, D. N. (2016). The legal status of suicide: A global review. International Journal of Law and Psychiatry, 44, 54–74. https://pubmed.ncbi.nlm.nih.gov/26375452/

Linehan, M. M. (1993). *Cognitive-behavioural treatment of borderline personality disorder.* Guilford Press.

Litz, B. T., Stein, N., Delaney, E., Lebowitz, L., Nash, W. P., Silva, C., & Maguen, S. (2009). Moral injury and moral repair in war veterans: A preliminary model and intervention strategy. *Clinical Psychology Review, 29*(8), 695–706.

Lupien, S. J., McEwen, B. S., Gunnar, M. R., & Heim, C. (2009). Effects of stress throughout the lifespan on the brain, behaviour and cognition. *Nature Reviews Neuroscience, 10*(6), 434–445. https://doi.org/10.1038/nrn2639

Malone, K. M., & McGuinness, S. (2009). *Study of suicide victims in Ireland* — more than 80% talked about ideas before death

Maslach, C., Jackson, S. E., & Leiter, M. P. (1997). Maslach Burnout Inventory: Third edition. In C. P. Zalaquett & R. J. Wood (Eds.), *Evaluating stress: A book of resources* (pp. 191–218). Scarecrow Education

Maté, G. (2008). *In the Realm of Hungry Ghosts: Close Encounters with Addiction.* North Atlantic Books.

Maté, G. (2023). *The Definition of Trauma and How We Can Fix Our Psychological Wounds* | EP 425. (2023, January 5). Spotify. Retrieved February 14, 2026, from https://open.spotify.com/episode/2Ud3ai7KbGLWOlityht55z

McEwen, B. S. (2017). Neurobiological and systemic effects of chronic stress. *Chronic Stress, 1*, 1–11. https://doi.org/10.1177/2470547017692328

McEwen, B. S., & Morrison, J. H. (2013). The brain on stress: Vulnerability and plasticity of the prefrontal cortex over the life course. *Neuron, 79*(1), 16–29. https://doi.org/10.1016/j.neuron.2013.06.028

McEwen, B. S. (2007). *Physiology and Neurobiology of Stress and Adaptation: Central Role of the Brain.* Cambridge University Press.

McGladrey, L. (2020). Combat and Operational Stress First Aid (retrieved from responderalliance.com)

McMains, M. J., Mullins, W. C., & Young, A. T. (2020). *Crisis negotiations: Managing critical incidents and hostage situations in law enforcement and corrections* (6th ed.). Routledge.

Michel, K., Jobes, D. A., & Berman, A. L. (2017). *Self-harm and suicide prevention: A collaborative clinical approach.* Hogrefe.

Michel, K., Jobes, D. A., & Shea, S. C. (2017). The Collaborative Assessment and Management of Suicidality (CAMS): An evolving evidence-based clinical approach. *American Journal of Psychotherapy, 71*(3), 1–9.

Mikulincer, M., & Shaver, P. R. (2012). An attachment perspective on psychopathology. *World Psychiatry, 11*(1), 11–15.

Mitchell, J. T. & Everly, G. S. (1996). Critical Incident Stress Debriefing(CISD): an operations manual for the prevention of traumatic stress among emergency services and disaster workers. Second edition, revised. Ellicott City, MD: Chevron Publishing.

Munch, E. (1893). *The Scream* [Painting]. National Gallery. https://www.nasjonalmuseet.no

Myers, M. W., & Hodges, S. D. (2009). Making it up and making do: Simulation, imagination, and empathic accuracy. In K. D. Markman, W. M. P. Klein, and J. A. Suhr (Eds.), *Handbook*

Nadler, A. (2002). Inter-group helping relations as power relations: Maintaining or challenging social dominance between groups through helping. Journal of Social Issues, 58(3), 487–502;

National Institute for Health and Care Excellence (NICE). (2022). *Autism spectrum disorder in adults: Diagnosis and management* (NG142).

Neff, K. D. (2012). The science of self-compassion. In C. K. Germer and R. D. Siegel (Eds.), *Wisdom and compassion in psychotherapy: Deepening mindfulness in clinical practice* (pp. 79–92). The Guilford Press.

Newman, K. M. (2020, August 18). How Journaling Can Help You in Hard Times. Greater Good. Retrieved January 18, 2026, from https://greatergood.berkeley.edu/article/item/how_journaling_can_help_you_in_hard_times

Ng, Y. P., & Panirselvam, R. R. (2021). Attempted suicide and the criminal justice system in a sample of forensic psychiatric patients in Malaysia. medRxiv. https://www.medrxiv.org/content/10.1101/2021.06.30.21259822v1.full

NIH (2025). *Cyberbullying linked with suicidal thoughts and attempts in young adolescents, 2025. National Institutes of Health.* Available at: https://www.nih.gov/news-events/nih-research-matters/cyberbullying-linked-suicidal-thoughts-attempts-young-adolescents (Accessed: 02 January 2026).

Nippon.com (2025). *The number of suicides decreased in Japan in 2024.* Available at: https://www.nippon.com/en/japan-data/h02293 (Accessed: 02 January 2026).

Nolen-Hoeksema S (1991). Responses to depression and their effects on the duration of depressive episodes. Journal of Abnormal Psychology, 100(4), 569. 10.1037/0021-843X.100.4.569

Norcross, J. C., & Wampold, B. E. (2011). Evidence-based therapy relationships: Research conclusions and clinical practices. *Psychotherapy, 48*(1), 98–102.

O'Connor, R. C. (2011). *Towards an Integrated Motivational–Volitional Model of Suicidal Behaviour.* In R. C. O'Connor et al. (Eds.), *International Handbook of Suicide Prevention.* Wiley-Blackwell

Ogden, P., Minton, K., & Pain, C. (2006). Trauma and the Body: *A Sensorimotor Approach to Psychotherapy.* W. W. Norton and Company.

Osafo, J., Akotia, C. S., Boakye, K. E., Andoh-Arthur, J., & Oppong Asante, K. (2024). To keep the law or to repeal it: Views of parliamentarians on the call to decriminalise attempted suicide in Ghana. PMC. https://pmc.ncbi.nlm.nih.gov/articles/PMC11017692/

Oxford Review (No date) *Cultural intelligence (CQ) - definition and explanation.* Available at: https://oxford-review.com/the-oxford-review-dei-diversity-equity-and-inclusion-dictionary/cultural-intelligence-cq-definition-and-explanation/ (Accessed: 02 January 2026).

Philippot, P., Chapelle, G. & Blairy, S. (2010, September 10). Respiratory feedback in the generation of emotion. Cognition and Emotion, 16(5), 605–627.

Post-traumatic stress disorder (PTSD) (2024) *Mayo Clinic.* Available at: https://www.mayoclinic.org/diseases-conditions/post-traumatic-stress-disorder/symptoms-causes/syc-20355967 (Accessed: 31 December 2025).

Prince. (1999). *Beautiful strange* [Song]. *On Rave Un2 the Joy Fantastic.* NPG Records.

Ramsland, K. (2012). Suicide Notes. [onlinc] Psychology Today. Available at: <https://www.psychologytoday.com/us/blog/shadow-boxing/201210/suicide-notes> [Accessed 1 October 2022].

Rock, P. L., Roiser, J. P., Riedel, W. J., & Blackwell, A. D. (2014). Cognitive impairment in depression: A systematic review and meta-analysis. *Psychological Medicine, 44*(10), 2029–2040. https://doi.org/10.1017/S0033291713002535

Rogers, A., Pilgrim, D., & Lacey, R. (2018). Experiencing mental health care: The importance of transparency and trust. *Social Science and Medicine, 212*, 38–45.

Rogers, C.R. (1957). The necessary and sufficient conditions of therapeutic personality change. *Journal of Consulting Psychology, 21*(2), 95–103.

Rogers, C. R., & Farson, R. E. (1957). Active listening. *Industrial Relations Centre of the University of Chicago.*

Rosenbaum, S. (2017). *Transformational listening: How listening can change organisations and relationships.* New York, NY: Routledge.

Rudd, M. D., Joiner, T., & Rajab, M. H. (2006). *Treating Suicidal Behaviour: An Effective, Time-Limited Approach.* Guilford Press.

Sagan, C. (1980). Cosmos. Random House.

Sagan, C. (1985). Contact. Simon and Schuster.

Saya, A., Albanesi, G., Cichetti, D., Di Molfetta, M., Guarino, Y., Niolu, C., & Siracusano, A. (2025). Notes on psychiatrist liability around the world regarding suicide. Frontiers in Psychiatry, 15, 1466325. https://pmc.ncbi.nlm.nih.gov/articles/PMC11799254/

Schon, D. A. (1991). The reflective practitioner. Ashgate Publishing.

Schwartz, R. C. (1995). *Internal Family Systems Therapy.* Guilford Press.

Seligman, M. E., & Maier, S. F. (1967). Failure to escape traumatic shock. *Journal of Experimental Psychology, 74*(1), 1–9. https://doi.org/10.1037/h0024514

Seppälä EM, Bradley C, Moeller J, Harouni L, Nandamudi D, & Brackett MA (2020). Promoting Mental Health and Psychological Thriving in University Students: A Randomised Controlled Trial of Three Well-Being Interventions. *Front. Psychiatry* 11:590. doi: 10.3389/fpsyt.2020.00590

Sharma, P. (2024). 8 common myths about suicide - Mayo Clinic Health System. Available at: https://www.mayoclinichealthsystem.org/hometown-health/speaking-of-health/8-common-myths-about-suicide (Accessed: 04 January 2026).

Shay, J. (2014). *Moral injury.* Psychoanalytic Psychology, 31(2), 182–191.

Sheftall, A. H., Schoppe-Sullivan, S. J., & Bridge, J. A. (2014). Insecure attachment and suicidal behaviour in adolescents. *Journal of Clinical Child and Adolescent Psychology, 43*(5), 699–712.

Shneidman, E. S. (1985). A definition of suicide. New York, NY: Wiley & Sons

Shneidman, E. S. (1993). *Suicide as Psychache: A Clinical Approach to Self-destructive Behaviour.* Jason Aronson.

Shneidman, E. S. (1996). *The Suicidal Mind.* Oxford University Press.

Shneidman, E.S. (2001). *Comprehending Suicide: Landmarks in 20th-Century Suicidology.* American Psychological Association.

Siegel, D. J. (1999). The Developing Mind: How Relationships and the Brain Interact to Shape Who We Are—New York: The Guildford Press.

Slavich, G. M. (2020). Social Safety Theory: A biologically based evolutionary perspective on life stress, health, and behaviour. Annual Review of Clinical Psychology, 16, 265–295. doi.org

Solomon, C. M., & Schell, M. S. (2009). Managing across cultures: the seven keys to doing business with a global mindset. New York, McGraw-Hill

Springtide. (2025, March 18). *Gen Alpha teens value openness about mental health - Springtide Research Institute.* Springtide

Research Institute. https://springtideresearch.org/post/mental-health/gen-alpha-teens-value-openness-about-mental-health

Stanley, B., & Brown, G. K. (2012). Safety planning intervention: A brief intervention to mitigate suicide risk. *Cognitive and Behavioural Practice, 19*(2), 256–264. https://doi.org/10.1016/j.cbpra.2011.01.001

Stanley, B., Brown, G. K., Brent, D. A., et al. (2018). Comparison of the safety planning intervention with follow-up telephone calls vs usual care after emergency department visits. *JAMA Psychiatry, 75*(9), 894–900. https://doi.org/10.1001/jamapsychiatry.2018.1776

Southwick, S. M., & Charney, D. S. (2012). *Resilience: The Science of Mastering Life's Greatest Challenges*. Cambridge University Press.

Subramaniam, M., et al. (2021). Recovery from past suicide attempts: Correlates of time since the last attempt in a national sample of adults. *Journal of Affective Disorders, 282*, 619–626.

Szmukler, G., Daw, R., & Callard, F. (2014). Mental health law and the UN Convention on the Rights of Persons with Disabilities. International Journal of Law and Psychiatry, 37(3), 245–252. https://pmc.ncbi.nlm.nih.gov/articles/PMC4024199/

Szmukler, G. (2020). Involuntary detention and treatment: Are we edging toward a 'paradigm shift'? Schizophrenia Bulletin, 46(2), 231–235. https://pmc.ncbi.nlm.nih.gov/articles/PMC7043056/

The Lancet. (2023). Punishing the tortured: Criminalisation of suicide. The Lancet, 401(10384), 1241. https://www.thelancet.com/journals/lancet/article/PIIS0140-6736(23)00764-X/fulltext

Theodore P. Beauchaine et al. (2020). ADHD, financial distress, and suicide in adulthood: DOI:10.1126/sciadv.aba1551

Torres, V. L. (2022). *The Turning Pointe.* Knopf Books for Young Readers.

Torres, V. L. (2025). *On the Wings of la Noche.* Knopf Books for Young Readers.

Triplett, N. (1898). *The dynamogenic factors in peacemaking and competition.* The American Journal of psychology, 9(4), 507-533

Turecki, G., Brent, D. A., Gunnell, D., O'Connor, R. C., Oquendo, M. A., Pirkis, J., & Stanley, B. H. (2019). Suicide and suicide risk. *Nature Reviews Disease Primers, 5,* 74. https://doi.org/10.1038/s41572-019-0121-0

Twenge, J. M., & Campbell, W. K. (2018). Associations between screen time and lower psychological well-being among children and adolescents: Evidence from a population-based study. *Preventive medicine reports, 12,* 271–283. https://doi.org/10.1016/j.pmedr.2018.10.003

UKSOBS. (2024). Practical concerns after a death by suicide: Inquests. https://uksobs.org/we-can-help/suicide-bereavement/practical-concerns/

United for Global Mental Health. (2025). Suicide decriminalisation: A practical advocacy guide. https://unitedgmh.org/suicide-decriminalisation/

Vadlamani, L. N., & Gowda, M. (2019). Practical implications of Mental Healthcare Act 2017: Suicide and suicide attempt. Indian Journal of Psychiatry, 61(Suppl 4), S750–S755. https://pmc.ncbi.nlm.nih.gov/articles/PMC6482674/

Vaknin, O., & Vered Ne'eman-Haviv. (2025). Beyond right and wrong: A New Theoretical Model for Understanding Moral Injury. *European Journal of Trauma & Dissociation,* 9(3), 100569–100569. https://doi.org/10.1016/j.ejtd.2025.100569

VanderWeele, T. J., Wortham, J. S., Carey, L. B., Case, B. W., Cowden, R. G., Duffee, C., Jackson-Meyer, K., Lu, F., Mattson, S. A., Padgett, R. N., Peteet, J. R., Rutledge, J., Symons, X., & Koenig, H. G. (2025). Moral trauma, moral distress, moral injury, and moral injury disorder: definitions and assessments. Frontiers in Psychology, 16. https://doi.org/10.3389/fpsyg.2025.1422441

van der Kolk, B. (2014). *The Body Keeps the Score: Brain, Mind, and Body in the Healing of Trauma*. Viking

Volk, A. A., Dane, A. V., & Marini, Z. A. (2014). *What is bullying? A theoretical redefinition.* Aggression and Violent Behaviour, 19(4), 327–343.

Voss, C. (2016). Never split the difference: negotiating as if your life depended on it. First edition. New York, HarperBusiness, an imprint of HarperCollins Publishers

Walker, G. (2008). ACR Conference, Austin, Texas, workshop

Watson, K. W., Barker, L. L., & Weaver, J. B. (1995). The listening styles profile (LSP-16): Development and validation. *International Journal of Listening, 9*(1), 1–15.

Weger, H., Castle Bell, G., Minei, E. M., & Robinson, M. C. (2014). The relative effectiveness of active listening in initial interactions. *International Journal of Listening, 28*(1), 13–31

Williams, J. M. G., Barnhofer, T., Crane, C., et al. (2005). Autobiographical memory specificity and emotional disorder. *Psychological Bulletin, 131*(1), 122–148.

Williamson, V., Stevelink, S. A. M., & Greenberg, N. (2020). Occupational moral injury and mental health: Systematic review and meta-analysis. *The British Journal of Psychiatry, 217*(6), 1–9.

Witt, K., Teo, S. M., Ziou, M., Rajaram, G., Baker, D. G., Browne, V., Schmaal, L., McGorry, P. D. & Gao, C. X. (2025). *Generational effects in self-reported age of onset for youth suicidal ideation, self-harm and attempted suicide: A retrospective analysis using data from the Australian National Study of Mental Health and Wellbeing, 2020-2022.* Australian & New Zealand Journal of Psychiatry 59(11), pp. 1035–1043. https://doi.org/10.1177/00048674251393162

World Health Organisation. (2014). *Preventing Suicide: A Global Imperative.* WHO Press

World Health Organisation. (2023). *Mental disorders.* https://www.who.int/news-room/fact-sheets/detail/mental-disorders

World Health Organisation. (2023). *Suicide* (Fact sheet). Retrieved from https://www.who.int/news-room/fact-sheets/detail/suicide 113 Zelfmoordpreventie

World Health Organization. (2025). World mental health today and mental health atlas 2024. https://www.who.int/news/item/02-09-2025-over-a-billion-people-living-with-mental-health-conditions-services-require-urgent-scale-up

World Health Organisation. (2023). Suicide (Fact sheet). Retrieved from https://www.who.int/news-room/fact-sheets/detail/suicide 113 Zelfmoordpreventie

Wu, K. C.-C., Cai, Z., Chang, Q., Chang, S.-S., Yip, P. S. F., & Chen, Y.-Y. (2022). Criminalisation of suicide and suicide rates: An ecological study of 171 countries in the world. BMJ Open, 12(2), e049425. https://pmc.ncbi.nlm.nih.gov/articles/PMC8860012/

Zajonc, R. B. & Sales, S. M. (1966). *Social facilitation of dominant and subordinate responses.* Journal of Experimental Social Psychology, 2 (2), 160–168.

Acknowledgements

Pascal would like to thank:
My co-authors: Sadiyah Reyal and Jasmine Garg

My family: Valerie Torres-Comvalius, Alex Comvalius, Nancy Comvalius, Serge Comvalius, Jolanda ten Brinke, Floor Comvalius, Madelief Comvalius, Mike Torres, Yvonne Torres and Vanessa Palensky

My friends: Roald Bakker, Angelo Schifano, Harry van Oers, Roger Huijgen, Jim Verschelden, Ruud van Oorschot, Arno Konings, Michael Bijtenhoorn, Gijs Buijsse, Jean-Christophe Barth-Coullaré, Amrah Minzar, Ashani Chawda, Chinmayi Patil, Yukta Chordia, Aparimita Tiwari, Meenal Maheshwari, Catherine Davidson, Sanyam Gupta, Tatiana Lukyanova, Linda Heng, Yi Chen Tsai and Thomas John

My cat: Amairin Kaya-San

Special thanks to:
1for2 Social innovation: Kirsten Heukels and Bas Kousemaker
Andrew Brown for writing the foreword of this book

All the students, mediators, negotiators, mental health professionals and trainers I met around the globe. This book would not be possible without your support and contribution in any form.

Jasmine would like to thank:

The honesty of the individuals whose experiences inspired these pages. Their names remain fictional to protect their privacy, but their courage and vulnerability shine through every story.

My parents: Over the years, they have come a long way—from once dismissing mental illness as a sham or a result of a poor lifestyle, to acknowledging that it is real and deserves compassion, professional help, and support. Watching that shift in perspective has meant more to me than I can put into words.

My friends who stood by me throughout this journey: Prabhjot Singh and Tushar Bansal, my school friends; Gauri Chuttani, Vaishnavi Gaur, Kunwarbir Singh and Sidharth Kapoor, my college friends. I am deeply grateful to them.

Finally, I would like to thank my co-author, Pascal. Since 2022, he has been both a friend and a mentor. At times when I struggled to stay afloat, he encouraged me to keep writing and helped me believe in my own voice. Despite his extensive experience as an author, a suicide prevention gatekeeper, and a professional in this field, he never made the idea of writing a book feel intimidating. Instead, he made it feel possible.

Sadiyah would like to thank:
Vanessa Torres and Kirsten Heukels for trusting me with their story. And, Pascal, for always believing in more than I ever did.

About the authors

Pascal Comvalius is a Communication Behaviour Specialist, an IMI-Certified Mediator, MFN-registered mediator, Certified Crisis & Hostage Negotiator, Certified Suicide Prevention Gatekeeper, Certified Confidential Counsellor, and an international managing partner at 1for2 Social Innovation. He earned a master's degree with merit in "Communication, Behaviour and Credibility Analysis" at Manchester Metropolitan University under the supervision of Professor Dawn Archer. Following mediation training in Holland and at Erickson Mediation Institute, Minneapolis, MN, Pascal undertook crisis and hostage negotiation training at PATC with Dr Andy Young, Jack Cambria, Andrew Brown, and Mark Lowther. He also completed levels I-IV of "Kinesic Interviewing and Interrogation" under the guidance of Stan Walters. His suicide prevention gatekeeper training was conducted at the 113 suicide prevention helpline organisation. He followed the forensic interview NICHD protocol course in the

Netherlands, which is designed to help children provide detailed, accurate accounts of events such as (sexual) abuse.

Pascal practices and teaches mediation, crisis negotiation, and credibility analysis worldwide at universities, organisations, and law enforcement agencies. He has served as a coach and judge at international mediation and negotiation competitions, including CDRC and the ICC. As a coach, he has won several awards coaching teams from universities in India and Sri Lanka. He is a former vice-president of the Academy of Professional Family Mediators (APFM) and a former member of the executive committee of the Independent Standards Commission of the International Mediation Institute. Currently, he holds the position of chairing the IMI appraisal committee. Pascal is also a visiting faculty member at Maharashtra National Law University in Mumbai, India, where he teaches for the master's degree in Mediation and Conflict Resolution. He is the author of the book "Mediation in Criminal Cases."

Jasmine Garg is an Advocate practising before the Punjab and Haryana High Court at Chandigarh and the District Courts of Chandigarh and Sangrur. Enrolled with the Bar in 2022, she has been actively engaged in litigation and dispute resolution throughout her legal career. Born and raised in Sangrur, Punjab, she later moved to Chandigarh to pursue a career in law. She holds a B.A. LL.B. (Hons.) from Panjab University, Chandigarh, and a Post Graduate Diploma in Alternative Dispute Resolution from NALSAR University of Law, Hyderabad. Jasmine is also an IMI-qualified mediator, reflecting her strong interest in collaborative and humane approaches to resolving disputes.

Known for her zestful approach to advocacy, Jasmine views the practice of law not merely as courtroom argument but as a responsibility toward the individuals whose lives are shaped by legal conflicts. Her work spans civil, constitutional, criminal, service, and commercial matters, involving legal research, drafting, and appearances before courts.

Alongside litigation, she has worked closely in mediation and arbitration, serving as a mediator and case officer for institutions involved in dispute resolution and online dispute resolution platforms. Through these roles, she has handled a wide variety of disputes, ranging from commercial and financial conflicts to matrimonial and employment matters. These experiences exposed her to the deeply human dimensions of conflict and reinforced her belief that law must always remain connected to empathy and understanding.

During her college years, Jasmine developed a deep interest in mental health and emotional well-being. Over time, this interest naturally intertwined with her legal career, as she witnessed how personal struggles, relationships, trauma, and resilience often lie beneath the legal disputes brought before courts and mediators.

Through her writing, Jasmine explores mental health not as an abstract subject but as a lived human experience. While some characters appear under fictional names, their emotions and struggles are rooted in real observations of vulnerability, courage, and the quiet ways people learn to heal.

She believes that conversations around mental health should be honest, compassionate, and free from stigma. Through this book, she hopes readers find recognition, understanding, and the reassurance that they are not alone in their struggles.

Sadiyah Reyal is an Attorney-at-Law (Sri Lanka) and holds an LL.B. (Hons) (First Class) and LL.M. (Hons) (Distinction) in International Business and Commercial Law. She previously served as a Research Officer at the Supreme Court of Sri Lanka. She currently works with the International Mediation Institute (IMI) on its Operations Team. Sadiyah is also a Senior Partner at Moot Court Bench, Sri Lanka, where she developed an International Commercial Mediation training curriculum and helped launch the world's first Investor–State ADR Competition. She regularly trains law students, professionals, and institutions in mediation and negotiation, including delivering programmes for organisations such as the Singapore Prison Service.

Internationally, she has both competed and coached at leading mediation competitions. She was ranked 5th globally at the 17th ICC International Commercial Mediation Competition (Paris). She later coached teams to multiple recognitions at the same competition, including Special Awards for Mediation Advocacy. At the IBA–VIAC CDRC Vienna Mediation and Negotiation Competition, she was named Champion Mediator in 2022 and subsequently coached a team to 1st Runner-Up in 2023.

About the foreword

Andrew B Brown

Chief Inspector (retd.) Andrew B Brown is an internationally renowned negotiator with specialist knowledge and experience in dealing with kidnap for ransom; in designing conflict de-escalation skills for military and humanitarian operations; and in acting as an expert witness to judicial inquiries into the response to hostage-taking. As a Fellow of the Chartered Management and Security Institutes, he has developed advanced negotiation and crisis leadership skills for major corporations, public bodies, and Olympic sports coaches. A Fulbright Alumnus, he continues to teach advanced negotiation tactics to many law enforcement agencies.

His doctoral studies and experience in Afghan & African kidnappings have led him to research, critique and advise NGOs on how to prepare, prevent and respond to the threat of international kidnap and abduction. As the Chief Security Officer for an INGO, he advises on safety and security for their overseas humanitarian missions in some of the world's most hostile environments on how to stay safe while educating, advocating, and accompanying many refugees and displaced people towards a better life.

He is newly appointed to the Board of Ranger Wellbeing, which focuses on supporting wildlife rangers with practical, culturally grounded safety & mental wellbeing training for the holistic development of those dedicating their lives to conservation.

Published in Modern Piracy & Maritime Terrorism: The Challenges of Piracy for the 21st Century and contributed chapters to the 5th & 6th Editions of Crisis Negotiations: Managing Critical Incidents and Hostage Situations in Law Enforcement & Corrections, he remains an Advisor to the Editorial Boards of the Criminal Psychology & Criminal Investigations, and the Crisis Response Journals.

Official Spotify Playlist:

www.ingramcontent.com/pod-product-compliance
Lightning Source LLC
Chambersburg PA
CBHW031338230926
51848CB00002B/282
9789465268217